"A provocative cultural analysis arguing that the Second Amendment and white supremacy are inextricably bound."
—*Kirkus Reviews*

"From an eminent scholar comes this timely and urgent intervention on U.S. gun culture. *Loaded* is a high-impact assault on the idea that Second Amendment rights were ever intended for all Americans. A timely antidote to our national amnesia about the white supremacist and settler colonialist roots of the Second Amendment."
—Caroline Light, author of *Stand Your Ground: A History of America's Love Affair with Lethal Self-Defense*

"*Loaded* recognizes the central truth about our 'gun culture': that the privileged place of guns in American law and society is the by-product of the racial and class violence that has marked our history from its beginnings."
—Richard Slotkin, author of *The Gunfighter Nation: Myth of the Frontier in Twentieth-Century America*

"*Loaded* is a masterful synthesis of the historical origins of violence and militarism in the United States. Roxanne Dunbar-Ortiz reminds us of what we've chosen to forget at our own peril: that from mass shootings to the routine deployment of violence against civilians by the U.S. military, American violence flows from the normalization of racialized violence in our country's founding history."
—Johanna Fernández, Assistant Professor of History at Baruch College of the City University of New York, author of the forthcoming book *When the World Was Their Stage: A History of the Young Lords Party, 1968–1976*

D0207522

"Just what did the founding fathers intend the Second Amendment to do? Roxanne Dunbar-Ortiz's answer to that question will unsettle liberal gun control advocates and open-carry aficionados alike. She follows the bloodstains of today's mass shootings back to the slave patrols and Indian Wars. There are no easy answers here, just the tough reckoning with history needed to navigate ourselves away from a future filled with more tragedies."

—James Tracy, co-author of *Hillbilly Nationalists, Urban Race Rebels and Black Power: Community Organizing in Radical Times*

"Gun violence, Roxanne Dunbar-Ortiz compellingly shows, is as U.S. American as apple pie. This important book peels back the painful and bloody layers of gun culture in the United States, and exposes their deep roots in the killing and dispossession of Native peoples, slavery and its aftermath, and U.S. empire-making. They are roots with which all who are concerned with matters of justice, basic decency, and the enduring tragedy of the U.S. love affair with guns must grapple."

—Joseph Nevins, author of *Dying to Live: A Story of U.S. Immigration in an Age of Global Apartheid*

"Roxanne Dunbar-Ortiz has done an outstanding job of resituating the so-called gun debate into the context of race and settler colonialism. The result is that the discussion about individual gun ownership is no longer viewed as an abstract moral question and instead understood as standing at the very foundation of U.S. capitalism. My attention was captured from the very first page."

—Bill Fletcher Jr., former president of TransAfrica Forum and syndicated writer

JAN 1 8

PRAISE FOR *LOADED: A DISARMING HISTORY
OF THE SECOND AMENDMENT*

"Roxanne Dunbar-Ortiz is a major spokesperson for what might be called the "new exceptionalism." Instead of viewing the United States as a model that other nations should imitate, a new generation of historians finds the United States to be a society founded on genocide, slavery and male domination, and permeated by hatred toward those who are different. In her earlier book, *An Indigenous Peoples' History of the United States*, Ortiz argued that the legacy of its Indian wars shaped the United States' military practices in, for example, the Philippines. Now, in *Loaded*, she widens her lens to propose that the addiction to violence characteristic of American domestic institutions also derives from the frontiersman's belief in solving problems by killing. Whether expressed in individual cruelty like the collection of scalps or group barbarism by settler colonialists calling themselves 'militias,' violence has become an ever-widening theme of life in the United States."

—Staughton Lynd

"For anyone who believes we need more than 'thoughts and prayers' to address our national gun crisis, *Loaded* is required reading. Beyond the Second Amendment, Roxanne Dunbar-Ortiz presents essential arguments missing from public debate. She forces readers to confront hard truths about the history of gun ownership—linking it to ongoing structures of settler colonialism, white supremacy, and racial capitalism. These are the open secrets of North American history. It is our anxious denial as much as our public policies that perpetrate violence. Only by coming to peace with our history can we ever be at peace with ourselves. This, for me, is the great lesson of *Loaded*."

—Christina Heatherton, co-editor of *Policing the Planet: Why the Policing Crisis Led to Black Lives Matter*

 Churchill County Library
553 S. Maine Street
Fallon, Nevada 89406
(775) 423-7581

"Roxanne Dunbar-Oritz's *Loaded* argues U.S. history is quint-essential gun history, and gun history is a history of racial terror and genocide. In other words, gun culture has never been about hunting. From crushing slave rebellions to Indigenous resistance, arming individual white settler men has always been the strategy for maintaining racial and class rule and for taking Indigenous land from the founding of the settler nation to the present. With clarity and urgency, Dunbar-Ortiz asks us not to think of our current moment as an exceptional era of mass-shootings. Instead, the very essence of the Second Amendment and the very project of U.S. 'settler democracy' has required immense violence that began with Indigenous genocide and has expanded to endless war-making across the globe. This is a must read for any student of U.S. history."

—Nick Estes, author of the forthcoming book *Our History Is the Future: Mni Wiconi and Native Liberation*

"Trigger warning! This is a superb and subtle book, not an intellectual safe space for confirming your preconceptions—whatever those might be—but rather a deeply necessary provocation. Roxanne Dunbar-Ortiz has done it again, giving us a fluid and sweeping history of the many painful contradictions that are the deep history of America's love–hate relationship with firearms. In understanding that history, *Loaded* also unpacks the contemporary pathologies of both fanatical gun culture and quixotic liberal moralizing against guns. As Dunbar-Ortiz shows us, the key connection between these antagonistic positions is their shared silence on that most pressing and persistent of American problems: economic exploitation and inequality."

—Christian Parenti, author of *Lockdown America: Police and Prisons in the Age of Crisis*

"More than a history of the Second Amendment, this is a powerful history of the forging of white nationalism and empire through racist and naked violence. Explosively, it also shows how even liberal—and some leftist—pop culture icons have been complicit in the myth-making that has shrouded this potent historical truth."

  —Gerarld Horne, author of *The Counter Revolution of 1776: Slave Resistance and the Origins of the USA*

"*Loaded* unleashes a sweeping and unsettling history of gun laws in the United States, beginning with anti-Native militias and anti-Black slave patrols. From the roots of white men armed to forge the settler state, the Second Amendment evolved as a tool for protecting white, male property owners. It's a must read for anyone who wants to uncover the long fetch of contemporary Second Amendment battles."

  —Kelly Lytle Hernandez, author of *City of Inmates: Conquest, Rebellion, and the Rise of Human Caging in Los Angeles, 1771–1965*

"Roxanne Dunbar-Ortiz provides a brilliant decolonization of the Second Amendment of the United States Constitution. She describes how the 'savage wars' against Indigenous Peoples, slave patrols (which policing in the U.S. originates from), today's mass shootings, and the rise in white nationalism are connected to the Second Amendment. This is a critically important work for all social science disciplines."

  —Michael Yellow Bird, professor and director of Tribal and Indigenous Peoples Studies at North Dakota State University

"There is no more interesting historian of the United States than Roxanne Dunbar-Ortiz. And with *Loaded* she has done it again, taking a topic about which so much has already been written, distilling it down, turning it inside out, and allowing us to see American history anew."
—Walter Johnson, author of *River of Dark Dreams: Slavery and Empire in the Mississippi Valley's Cotton Kingdom*

"In her trenchant analysis of the Second Amendment, Dunbar-Ortiz avoids a legalistic approach and eschews the traditional view that links the amendment to citizens' need to protect themselves from a tyrannical government. . . . [Her] argument will be disturbing and unfamiliar to most readers, but her evidence is significant and should not be ignored."
—*Publishers Weekly*

LOADED

A Disarming History
of the Second Amendment

Roxanne Dunbar-Ortiz

City Lights Books | San Francisco

Copyright © 2018 by Roxanne Dunbar-Ortiz

All Rights Reserved.

The Open Media Series is edited by Greg Ruggiero.

Cover design by Herb Thornby

Library of Congress Cataloging-in-Publication Data
Names: Dunbar-Ortiz, Roxanne, 1939- author.
Title: Loaded : a disarming history of the Second Amendment /
Roxanne Dunbar
   Ortiz.
Description: San Francisco : City Lights Books, [2017] | Includes
   bibliographical references and index.
Identifiers: LCCN 2017037851 (print) | LCCN 2017045903 (ebook)
   | ISBN 9780872867239 (paperback) | ISBN 9780872867246 (ebook)
Subjects: LCSH: Firearms ownership—United States—History. |
United States.
   Constitution. 2nd Amendment—History. | Firearms—Law and
   legislation—United States—History. | Firearms and crime—United
   States—History. | United States—Militia—History.
Classification: LCC HV7436 (ebook) | LCC HV7436 .D86 2017
(print) | DDC
   323.4/3—dc23
LC record available at https://lccn.loc.gov/2017037851

City Lights Books are published at the City Lights Bookstore
261 Columbus Avenue, San Francisco, CA 94133
www.citylights.com

I could never again raise my voice against the violence of the oppressed in the ghettos without having first spoken clearly to the greatest purveyor of violence in the world today—my own government.

> —Martin Luther King, Jr., April 4, 1967 speech at
> Riverside Church, New York City

CONTENTS

GUN LOVE

In the summer of 1970, while I was living and organizing in New Orleans with a women's study action group, we discovered that our group had been infiltrated. One of the volunteers who had come to work with our project six months earlier was secretly making detailed reports of our meetings, but with distortions and outright lies, using terms like "extreme," "fanatic," "potentially violent." We were aware that she was a Social Work graduate student at Brandeis University, but had no idea we were the topic of her dissertation or that she was associated with the government-funded Lamberg Center for the Study of Violence. She had also lied to us about her background, claiming that she came from a single-parent family with a working mother in Mobile, Alabama. We had not checked out her history, but it only took one phone call to learn that she came from a wealthy, social register Mobile family. When confronted, she appeared earnestly sorry and tried to convince us that she had been required to report on us in order to continue receiving her stipend, without which she supposedly could not continue her studies at the university.

After her departure, we became caught up in a current of repression and paranoia. One or two or three pale blue New Orleans police cars parked across the street from our building every day. The cops took pictures, and a suspicious, unmarked car with Illinois plates followed us. Older local activists told us the cars' occupants were "red squad" detectives from the Chicago Police Department. We installed a heavy lock on the flimsy wooden door to our run-down building, but we did not feel safe.

After a week of heavy police surveillance, we began receiving telephone calls from a man claiming to be a member of the Ku Klux Klan. The man threatened to burn down our building, and, of course, we didn't trust the police, so we did not report it. Instead, we decided to arm ourselves. We saw it as a practical step, not a political act, something we needed for self-defense in order to continue working, not at all embracing armed struggle, which our group opposed as a strategy for making change in the United States. We knew that law enforcement authorities would think twice about attacking us if they knew we were armed. In reality, we were joining a trend occurring in movement groups across the country at that time, and once armed, our mindsets changed to match the new reality.

Two of us drove across the Lake Ponchartrain Causeway to a gun show that was held weekly in a large tin shed on the Slidell fairgrounds. The pickups and vans of traveling gun dealers, with license plates from a dozen states, were parked around the site; I had a cousin in Oklahoma who made his living selling guns that way. Inside the shed, the scene was festive, like any ordinary weekend craft fair or flea market. There were children running and playing, older women sitting on folding chairs visiting with each other, younger women clutching infants and staying close to their men, vendors hawking wares and bargaining, Confederate battle flags waving. Everyone was white. We had no trouble finding the used 9mm automatics we sought. We chose three used Brownings for $100 each, clips included, and a case of military surplus ammunition.

"We're looking for a shotgun, too," I said to the dealer.

"For protection or duck huntin'?" the vendor asked.

"Protection."

He offered us a Mossberg 500 12-gauge police special riot gun, with a short barrel.

"Isn't it illegal to have this weapon?" I asked.

"Ain't a sawed-off, legal as taxes."

We bought it, along with some buckshot shells, all for cash. No paperwork required. The man who sold us the guns also had for sale a number of swastikas in various forms—pins, arm patches, photographs.

We went to the Tulane Law Library to research Louisiana gun laws and found that there were no gun laws in Louisiana. The only restriction was against building an arsenal—defined as more than twenty automatic or semiautomatic weapons—for illegal purposes. Carrying concealed and loaded weapons within the state with no registration was entirely legal. Federal laws prohibited transporting firearms across state lines for sale or to commit a crime, possession of stolen weapons, removal of serial numbers, and various foreign weapons, such as the AK-47.

We kept the loaded shotgun at the door, and we joined

an indoor shooting gallery at Lafayette Square. We practiced with the Brownings every day. Shotguns weren't allowed at the shooting club, but a shotgun took no skill to fire, only nerve and a steady shoulder. Soon after, we acquired rifles and joined a rifle club in the West Bank area. We loaded the bed of our station wagon with four M-1s, a Winchester .22, a .30-30 with a scope, and the riot shotgun, all purchased at the gun shows in Slidell. We paid for membership in the National Rifle Association and affixed their red and black emblem to the back window of the car. Cops were known to not stop vehicles with the stickers, although that probably didn't work for African Americans.

We acquired more small arms and went daily to the Lafayette Square pistol shooting gallery to practice. In addition to the Brownings, we now owned a snub-nosed Smith & Wesson .357, an S&W long-barrel .38, a Walther PPK 9mm, a Colt .45, and a Beretta .32 automatic. We'd purchased all the weapons legally and anonymously at gun shows. We soon had a closet full of guns, plus our new shotgun reloading equipment and a 100-pound bag of gunpowder.

We spent hours every day breaking down, cleaning, oiling, and polishing our weapons. We took turns loading shotgun shells. We had fallen under the spell of guns. Our relationship to them had become a kind of passion that was inappropriate to our political objectives, and it ended up distorting and determining them.

Knowing that the FBI intercepted our mail, and wanting to inform authorities that we were fully armed, I wrote to my father about my new hobbies—guns and gunsmithing.

Ironically, it seemed the first thing I'd done in my life that he really understood and supported.

"When you can shoot a squirrel in the eye with a .22 at forty yards on the first shot, you'll be a shooter," he wrote.

He must have been pleasantly surprised, because he knew that as a child I was terrified of his Remington .22 rifle and shotgun; I got it from my mother, who hated guns. I never asked her why, but she put the fear and hate in my sister and me. Notwithstanding her objections, my two older brothers followed our father. At adolescence, each one started hunting and brought home game, which was our major meat item. We were poor, and ammunition was expensive, so they all had to be good shots, practicing on bottles and cans with BB guns for years before they handled real firearms. It was all for hunting, practical, but there was that other element I could detect but not explain, until I fell in love with guns.

Gun-love can be akin to non-chemical addictions like gambling or hoarding, either of which can have devastating effects, mainly economic, but murder, suicide, accidental death, and mass shootings result only from guns. Guns are made for killing, and while nearly anything, including human hands, may be used to kill, only the gun is created for the specific purpose of killing a living creature. The sheer numbers of guns in circulation, and the loosening of regulations on handguns especially, facilitate deadly spur-of-the-moment reflex acts. *The Trace*, a nonprofit news organization focused on gun violence found that cases of road rage involving a firearm have more than doubled in two years, from 247 in 2014 to 620 in 2016. Research from

Gunwatch suggests that "more guns in more cars may simply equate to more road rage incidents in which a gun was brandished, or fired."[1]

At the time of my gun-love, which lasted about two years in the early 1970s, approximately half of all homes in the United States contained a weapon—112 million in total—but nearly a half century later, only a third of households contained firearms, which sounds like progress.[2] Yet the number of guns privately owned in the United States had reached more than 300 million, a number equal to the total population. The reality is that in the early twenty-first century, each gun owner possessed an average of eight guns.

It seems that our group, and others, during the years that the Vietnam War was playing out live on our televisions, were in the vanguard of a trend of owning multiple weapons. Army and Navy surplus clothing accompanied the trend, which was soon replaced by sweatshop-produced camouflage garb to meet consumer demand. Something else was also at work, which will be probed in the following chapters.

In 1970, at the time of my own gun phase, the then-celebrated U.S. historian Richard Hofstadter coined the term *gun culture*. "Many otherwise intelligent Americans cling with pathetic stubbornness to the notion that the people's right to bear arms is the greatest protection of their individual rights and a firm safeguard of democracy—without being in the slightest perturbed by the fact that no other democracy in the world observes any such 'right' and that in some democracies in which citizens' rights are rather better protected than in ours, such as England and the Scandinavian countries, our arms control policies would be considered laughable."[3]

Hofstadter narrates the historical roots that might explain the violence wrought by civilian gun use, but argues that other European countries were surely as violent. In one brief paragraph, he dismisses the Second Amendment as having any validity in constitutional law: "By its inclusion in the Bill of Rights, the right to bear arms thus gained permanent sanction in the nation, but it came to be regarded as an item on the basic list of guarantees of individual liberties. Plainly it was not meant as such. The right to bear arms was a collective, not an individual, right, closely linked to the civic need for 'a well regulated Militia.' It was, in effect, a promise that Congress would not be able to bar the states from doing whatever was necessary to maintain well-regulated militias."[4]

Did Hofstadter believe that these astute "founding fathers" mistakenly threw in the Second Amendment to a Bill of Rights that was about individual rights? Hofstadter does note, without discussion, that the first draft of the Virginia Constitution of 1776—Thomas Jefferson's work, which preceded the writing of the U.S. Constitution by nine years—included the individual right to bear arms, stating: "No freeman shall ever be debarred the use of arms." Did Jefferson make a mistake in Virginia, and then contribute to another mistake, making the right to bear arms an individual right in the U.S. Constitution? Hofstadter attributes these "flaws" in Jefferson and the other founders to "reverting to one of the genial fictions . . . the ancient Saxon militia."

Killing, looting, burning, raping, and terrorizing Indians were traditions in each of the colonies long before the Constitutional Convention. "Militias," as in government-controlled units, were institutionalized by Article I, Section 8, Clause 15 of the U.S. Constitution, and were used to officially invade and occupy Native land. But the Second Amendment (like the other ten amendments) enshrined an individual right. The Second Amendment's language specifically gave individuals and families the right to form volunteer militias to attack Indians and take their land.

Asserting this scattershot guess about the origin of the Second Amendment, Hofstadter offers no tie-in between this genealogy and the astronomical number of guns possessed in this country. So he settles on the National Rifle Association: "American legislators have been inordinately responsive to the tremendous lobby maintained by the National Rifle Association, in tandem with gunmakers and importers, military sympathizers, and far-right organizations. A nation that could not devise a system of gun control after its experiences of the 1960s [referring to the assassinations of President John F. Kennedy, Martin Luther King Jr., and Robert Kennedy], and at a moment of profound popular revulsion against guns, is not likely to get such a system in the calculable future. One must wonder how grave a domestic gun catastrophe would have to be in order to persuade us. How far must things go?"

Hofstadter's argument is important, not just because he was an influential liberal historian of the United States who penned the classic 1964 essay "The Paranoid Style in American Politics," but because his arguments about guns in 1970 have been used and repeated, like a mantra, ever since. Then, as now, gun-rights advocates and gun-control advocates have little basis for communicating. The great divide reflects, rather remarkably, the persistence of pro-gun narratives that have morphed as times changed over two centuries, from westward expansion, industrialization, and urbanization, to the advent of movies, television, and the Internet. Gun ownership appears irrational if not insane to gun-control advocates, while gun lovers rely on the Second Amendment, because they have no other argument and don't wish to admit, perhaps even to themselves, what the Second Amendment signifies. Neither party seems to have any idea what the Second Amendment was originally about, although many who "cling to their guns"[5] intuit why.

This blind spot, as well as the racism and erasure of history, can be seen in the following example. After retiring, the late Warren E. Burger, who served as the fifteenth chief justice of the United States from 1969 to 1986, wrote a long and impassioned plea for gun control, arguing that the Second Amendment was dated and no longer valid. Significantly, he published his commentary in *Parade* magazine, not a law journal. "Let's look at the history," Burger wrote. "First, many of the 3.5 million people living in the 13 original Colonies depended on wild game for food, and a good many of them required firearms for their defense from marauding Indians."[6]

There is no doubt that the United States is exceptional among wealthy nations—and even many poorer nations—in legal permissiveness about gun ownership, as well as in gun deaths per capita. By 2016, nearly all the states allowed open carry for firearms with various limitations regarding licensing, loaded or unloaded, weapons training or not, gun types, and so on. The holdouts not allowing open carry were California, Illinois, Florida, and the District of Columbia. Massachusetts, Minnesota, and New Jersey allow open carry for handguns but prohibit open carry of long guns, while New York and South Carolina allow open carry for long guns but prohibit open carry for handguns.[7]

Total gun deaths in the United States average around 37,000 a year, with two-thirds of those deaths being suicides, leaving approximately 12,000 homicides, a thousand of those at the hands of the police.[8] Mass shootings—ones that leave four or more people wounded or dead—now occur in the United States, on average, at the pace of one or more *per day*.[9] Disturbing as that fact is, mass shootings currently account for only 2 percent of gun killings annually.[10] The number of gun deaths—37,000—is roughly equal to death-by-vehicle incidents in the United States per year. To lawfully drive a vehicle, a person must acquire and maintain a driver's license and drive a car that is registered and insured. A car owner may be fined for driving with a visible safety flaw on the vehicle, such as a taillight out, and a driver may be stopped at any time by authorities and can easily lose the right to drive, among other restrictions. The high rate of traffic fatalities begs the question of how effective gun restrictions would be. Heavy drinking while driving causes nearly three times as many deaths as guns each year in the United States, despite restrictions on the buying, selling, and public use of alcohol. It is necessary to look elsewhere for what causes firearms proliferation and gun deaths; it is necessary to seek out the historical roots.

With the election of Bill Clinton in 1992, the Democratic Party platform for the first time included gun control, while the Republican Party platform opposed gun control, proclaiming: "We note that those who seek to disarm citizens in their homes are the same liberals who tried to disarm our Nation during the Cold War and are today seeking to cut our national defense below safe levels."[11] In the previous three presidential elections, neither the Republican Party nor Democratic Party platforms had mentioned guns at all.

With the Democrats in control of the White House and Congress in 1993, there was no trouble passing a gun-control bill requiring background checks, commonly called the "Brady Bill" after Jim Brady, who was wounded and permanently disabled during the shooting of President Ronald Reagan in 1981. Brady's wife, Sarah, had campaigned tirelessly for background checks, which did result in a bill that was introduced in Congress in 1987, but the measure lingered without action until it was signed into law in 1993. The following year, Congress passed a ban on assault weapons but in 2004, when the statute was up for renewal, it was allowed to lapse, as it had proved largely ineffectual and unenforceable. Georgetown University law professor David Cole writes: "It is remarkably difficult to define an 'assault weapon.' They are semiautomatic, which means they fire a new bullet with each trigger pull, while automatically reloading. But most guns made today are semiautomatic, so the ban on assault weapons focused on the cosmetic military appearance of certain guns, and was easily evaded by alterations in design. Moreover, while gun-rights proponents are hard-pressed to offer a legitimate reason for civilians to own assault weapons, they are used in a very small proportion of gun crimes. Most crimes involve ordinary handguns."[12]

Professor Cole finds a common thread of arguments condemning the National Rifle Association and does not question the organization's powerful role, which relies on a strong electoral base throughout the country, but issues this caution:

> Gun control advocates will not make progress until they recognize that the NRA's power lies in the appeal of its ideas, its political engagement and acumen, and the intense commitments of its members. Until gun control advocates can match these features, they are unlikely to make much progress. That the gun industry may have helped construct modern gun culture does not negate the very real power that culture holds today.[13]

Indeed, the N.R.A. has around 5 million dues-paying members, and many millions more who support N.R.A. calls for legislative action. The N.R.A. annual budget is $300 million, only 10 percent of which goes to direct lobbying. The N.R.A. does little lobbying, but rather follows and grades every political candidate on gun rights and calls for supporting or campaigning against the candidate accordingly; it focuses on state legislators, who make most gun laws; gun-rights activists tend to focus on Congress. The N.R.A. has active affiliates in many communities in every state, with an average membership of 100,000 per state.

While Cole recommends that we look for the reasons

why guns have such strong appeal in the United States in comparison with other societies, he does not explore those reasons. That is the purpose of this book. However, instead of dismissing the Second Amendment as antiquated and irrelevant, or as not actually meaning what it says, I argue that understanding the *purpose* of the Second Amendment is key to understanding the gun culture of the United States, and possibly the key to a new consciousness about the lingering effects of settler-colonialism and white nationalism.

The Second Amendment of the United States Constitution is a simple statement: *A well regulated militia being necessary to the security of a free State, the right of the People to keep and bear arms shall not be infringed.* The National Rifle Association and its constituency argue that the Second Amendment guarantees the right for every individual to bear arms, while gun-control advocates maintain, as did Hofstadter, that the Second Amendment is about states continuing to have their own militias—emphasizing the language of "well regulated"—and that this is manifest in the existing National Guard.[14]

However, the respective state militias were already authorized by the U.S. Constitution when the amendment was added. The Constitution recognized the existing colonial, now state, militias that formed before and during the War for Independence, and mandated to them vital roles to play: "to execute the Laws of the Union, suppress Insurrections and repel Invasion" (Article I, Section 8, Clause 15). The President of the United States is the commander-in-chief of the state militias "when called into the actual Service of the United States" (Article II, Section 2).[15]

Given that what are now the states' National Guards are descended from state militias, which themselves were repurposed from colonial militias, why was the Second Amendment added as one of the enumerated rights of man in the Bill of Rights? Unequivocally, the Second Amendment, along with the other nine amendments, constituted individual rights, and the militias referenced are voluntary, not state militias.

One argument that runs through historical accounts of the thinking behind the Second Amendment is the one Hofstadter settled on, that Thomas Jefferson romanticized old English-Saxon rural militias, idealizing his "yeoman" farmers as fiercely independent and rightly fearing Big Brother government, insisting on settlers' right to overthrow oppressive regimes. But, what colonists considered oppressive was any restriction that British authorities put on them in regard to obtaining land. In the instances of Bacon's Rebellion in 1676,[16] the War of Independence itself, and many cases in between, the settlers' complaint was the refusal of the British colonial authorities to allow them to seize Native land peripheral to the colonies, which could lead to unnecessary and expensive war. Historian Charles Sellers wrote: "Cheap land, held absolutely under the seaboard market's capitalist conception of property, swelled patriarchal honor to heroic dimensions in rural America. The father's authority rested on his legal title to the family land. Where European peasant landholdings were usually encumbered with obligations to some elite, the American farmer held in fee simple. Supreme in his domain, he was beyond interference by any earthly power.

Except for a modest tax and an occasional half-day of neighborhood roadwork or carousing militia drill, he owed no obligations of labor, money, service, or (finally) religious fealty to any person or entity. Fee-simple land, the augmenting theater of the patriarchal persona, sustained his honor and untrammeled will. This extraordinary independence inflated American farmers' conception of their class far above peasantry."[17]

In the pages ahead I explore various ways in which a dangerous gun culture has emerged in the United States, one that has entitled white nationalism, racialized dominance, and social control through violence. This book is a history of the Second Amendment's connection to that culture, and a reflection on how the violence it has spawned has deeply influenced the character of the United States.

Chapter One provides the historical context for understanding the Second Amendment's role in allowing settlers to control Black populations—enslaved and free—and the total war that settlers were waging against Indigenous Peoples to dispossess them of their land.

Chapter Two examines the fact that the Second Amendment granted rights to individual settlers to combat Native communities, and how doing so was part of a "savage war" that aided the territorial expansion of the United States throughout the continent and into the Caribbean and Pacific.

Chapter Three discusses the provisions of the Second Amendment that mandated every citizen, slaver or not, to capture and return people caught escaping from slavery; and how the amendment gave slavers the power to organize voluntary militias to help enforce slavery.

Chapter Four explores the role of Missouri pro-slavery guerrillas, most notably William Quantrill's "raiders," among whom were Jesse James and his brother Frank, and the Younger brothers, ruthless mass murderers who became iconic national celebrities and who were often portrayed as Robin Hood outlaws. Their use of pistols while riding became the hallmark of subsequent Wild West narratives that commercialized gun violence through pulp fiction, Hollywood films, television programming, and toys that led generations of children to play "cowboys and Indians" with imitation six-shooters.

Chapter Five explores the manner in which mythology surrounding "the hunter" has served to mask the historical purpose of the Second Amendment, and how narratives about settlers on unceded Indian land, like those about Daniel Boone, romanticized notions about gun use at a time when the United States was committing genocide against Native Americans.

Chapter Six explores the implications of the way that many in the United States see the Constitution as a sacred text from which flows the equally sacred and inviolable right to bear arms.

Chapter Seven traces the increase of mass shootings in the United States and the parallel rise of organized gun-rights advocacy as a reaction to national movements for civil rights and Black Power.

Chapter Eight tracks the revival and rise of white nationalist groups and militias.

Chapter Nine explores resistance to understanding the historical connections between the Second Amendment and white nationalism. The linkage is strongly resisted by anti-gun activists, including public officials, and simply denied by most pro-gun advocates.

As a whole, this book attempts to confront fundamental aspects of U.S. history that continue to be too often overlooked or denied, and which can be traced back to the original meaning and intention of the Second Amendment. It aims to confront the violence implicit in U.S. society from the moment of its conception, and the various narratives and forces that have taken shape to deny the consequences of that violence by popularizing and commercializing it. The book also aims to acknowledge the families, traditions, memories, and resistance of Indigenous People and African Americans whose lands and lives the Second Amendment was forged to take.

ONE

HISTORICAL CONTEXT OF THE SECOND AMENDMENT

The Anglo-American settlers' violent break from Britain in the late eighteenth century paralleled their search-and-destroy annihilation of Delaware, Cherokee, Muskogee, Seneca, Mohawk, Shawnee, and Miami, during which they slaughtered families without distinction of age or gender, and expanded the boundaries of the thirteen colonies into unceded Native territories.

The Declaration of Independence of 1776 symbolizes the beginning of the "Indian Wars" and "westward movement" that continued across the continent for another century of unrelenting U.S. wars of conquest. That was the goal of independence, with both the seasoned Indian killers of the Revolutionary Army and white settler-rangers/militias using extreme violence against Indigenous noncombatants with the goal of total domination. These forces were met with resistance movements and confederations identified with leaders such as Buckongeahelas of the Delaware; Alexander McGillivray of the Muskogee-Creek, Little Turtle and Blue Jacket of the Miami-Shawnee alliance; Joseph Brant of the Mohawk; and Cornplanter of the Seneca, as well as the great Tecumseh and the Shawnee-led confederation in the Ohio Valley. Without their sustained resistance, the intended genocide would have been complete; the eastern half of the continent was "ethnically cleansed" of Native nations by 1850, through forced relocation to "Indian Territory" west of the Mississippi.

The program of expansion and the wars against Native American civilization and the agricultural societies of the vast valley of the Ohio River and the Great Lakes region began before the Declaration with the French and Indian War of 1754–1763,[1] which was the North American extension of the Seven Years' War between France and Britain in Europe. Britain's victory over France in 1763 led to its domination of world trade, sea power, and colonial holdings for nearly two centuries. In the Treaty of Paris, France ceded Canada and all claims east of the Mississippi to Britain. In the course of that war, Anglo-American settlers intensified their use of counterinsurgent violence, which the Anglo settler elite dubbed "savage wars," against Indigenous peoples' resistance to their incursions into the territories of the Ottawa, Miami, Kickapoo, and the confederations identified with Pontiac's leadership of the Great Lakes region, spreading to the Illinois and Ohio countries. By the end of the war, significant numbers of Anglo settlers had taken Indigenous lands beyond the colonies' boundaries, and land speculation was a road to riches for a fortunate few.

To the settlers' dismay, soon after the 1763 Treaty of Paris was signed, King George III issued a proclamation prohibiting British settlement west of the Allegheny-

Appalachian mountain chain, ordering those who had settled there to relinquish their claims and return to the kingdom's thirteen colonies. Soon it became clear that the British authorities needed far more soldiers to enforce the edict, as thousands of settlers ignored it and continued to pour over the mountains, squatting on Indigenous lands, forming armed militias, and provoking Indigenous resistance. In 1765, in order to enforce the Proclamation line, the British Parliament imposed the Stamp Act on the colonists, a tax on all printed materials that had to be paid in British pounds, not local paper money. The iconic colonial protest slogan "taxation without representation is tyranny" marked the surge of rebellion against British control but it did not tell the whole story, considering what the tax was for: to pay the cost of housing, feeding, and transporting soldiers to contain and suppress the colonies from expanding further into Indian territory. The complaints iterated in the Declaration largely focus on the measures used by King George to prevent his rebellious subjects from grabbing more land: "[King George] has excited domestic Insurrections [slave revolts] amongst us, and has endeavoured to bring on the Inhabitants of our Frontiers, the merciless Indian Savages [Indigenous nations resisting genocidal wars], whose known Rule of Warfare, is an undistinguished Destruction, of all Ages, Sexes and Conditions."

By the early 1770s, terrorism waged by Anglo-American settlers against even Christianized Native communities within the colonies, and violent encroachment on those outside the colonial boundaries, raged, and illegal speculation in stolen Indian lands was rampant. In the southern colonies especially, farmers who had lost their land in competition with larger, more efficient, slave-worked plantations rushed for Native farmlands over the mountain range. These militant settlers—"rangers"—thus created the framework for the United States to appropriate Native territories and attempt to eradicate Indigenous nations across the continent for the following century. Illegal squatter-settlers, always with practiced Indian killers in the lead, initially depended on colonial militias for support; after the War of Independence they relied on the U.S. military to protect their settlements. During the war years of 1774–1783, the secessionists' parallel wars against Native nations were, in military historian John Grenier's words, "waypoints in the development of the first way of war. In them, we find the same elements— necessity and efficiency, the uncontrollable momentum of extravagant violence, and the quest for the subjugation of Indians—that had defined the first way of war throughout the colonial period."[2]

In a book first published in 1876 but written decades earlier, historian Joseph Doddridge (1769–1826), a minister and early settler in the Ohio Country, wrote:

> The early settlers on the frontiers of this country were like Arabs of the desert of Africa, in at least two respects; every man was a soldier, and from early in the spring till late in the fall, was almost continually in arms. Their work was often carried on by parties, each one of whom had his rifle and everything else belonging to his wardress. These were deposited in some central place in the field. A

sentinel was stationed on the outside of the fence, so that on the least alarm the whole company repaired to their arms, and were ready for combat in a moment.[3]

The Second Amendment thus reflects this dependence on individual armed men, not just in terms of a right to bear arms, but also as a *requirement* to bear arms, which was crucial to the integrity of the state and the conception of security achieved through a relationship between state and citizen.

In 1783, the British withdrew from the fight to maintain sovereignty over their thirteen colonies, not due to military defeat, but rather in order to redirect their resources to occupy and colonize South Asia. Britain's transfer of its claim to Indian Country west of the colonies spelled a nightmarish disaster for all Indigenous peoples east of the Mississippi, and ultimately all of North America that would be claimed and occupied by the United States. Britain's withdrawal in 1783 opened a new chapter of unrestrained racist violence and colonization of the continent.

The creation of the United States Constitution began in 1785, but the document was not approved by all the states and in effect until 1791. Meanwhile, the interim Continental Congress got to work on a plan for colonization over the mountain range. The Land Ordinance of 1785 established a centralized system for surveying and distributing land, with seized Native lands being auctioned off to the highest bidder. The "Northwest" (referring to the Ohio country) Ordinance of 1787 set forth a colonization procedure for annexation via military occupation, transforming to civilian territorial status under federal control, and finally, state-hood. These were the first laws of the incipient republic, revealing the motive for those desiring independence. It was the blueprint for the taking of the North American conti-nent, with lines of future settlement reaching the Pacific on the maps. The maps contained in the land ordinances, which laid out land in marketable square-mile plots, were not new; they were the products of pre-Revolutionary co-lonial elites, including George Washington, who as leader of the Virginia militia took armed surveying teams illegally into Ohio country, making him one of the most successful land speculators in the colonies. The wealthiest colonists were all speculators; acquiring land and enslaving people provided the very basis of the economy of the first nation born as a capitalist state, and by 1850, it was the wealthiest economy in the world.

In 1801, President Thomas Jefferson aptly described the new settler-state's intentions for horizontal and vertical continental expansion as an "empire for liberty," stating: "However our present interests may restrain us within our own limits, it is impossible not to look forward to distant times, when our rapid multiplication will expand itself be-yond those limits and cover the whole northern, if not the southern continent, with a people speaking the same lan-guage, governed in similar form by similar laws." This vi-sion of Manifest Destiny found form a few years later in the Monroe Doctrine, signaling the intention of annexing or dominating former Spanish colonial territories in the Amer-icas and the Pacific, which would be put into practice during the rest of the century, while carrying out brutal wars of extermination and expulsion of Native peoples to complete the continental shape of the United States today.

Taking land by force was not an accidental or spontaneous project or the work of a few rogue characters. The violent appropriation of Native land by white settlers was seen as an individual right in the Second Amendment of the U.S. Constitution, second only to freedom of speech. Male colonial settlers had long formed militias for the purpose of raiding and razing Indigenous communities and seizing their lands and resources, and the Native communities fought back. Virginia, the first colony, forbade any man to travel unless he was "well armed." A few years later, another law required men to take arms with them to work and to attend church or be fined. In 1658, the colony ordered every settler home to have a functioning firearm, and later even provided government loans for those who could not afford to buy a weapon. Similarly, New England colonial governments made laws such as the 1632 requirement that each person have a functioning firearm plus two pounds of gunpowder and ten pounds of bullets. Householders were fined for missing or defective arms and ammunition. No man was to appear at a public meeting unarmed.[4]

These laws stayed on the books of the earliest colonies and were created in new colonies as they were founded. The Second Amendment, ratified in 1791, enshrined these obligations as constitutional law: "A well regulated Militia, being necessary to the security of a free State, the right of the people to keep and bear Arms, shall not be infringed." The continuing significance of that "freedom" specified in the Bill of Rights reveals the settler-colonialist cultural roots of the

United States that appear even in the present as a sacred right. Several of the colonies that declared independence in 1776—Massachusetts, New Hampshire, New Jersey, Pennsylvania, Vermont, and Virginia—had already adopted individual gun-rights measures into their state constitutions before the Second Amendment was passed at the federal level.

Settler-militias and armed households were institutionalized for the destruction and control of Native peoples, communities, and nations. With the expansion of plantation agriculture, by the late 1600s they were also used as "slave patrols," forming the basis of the U.S. police culture after enslaving people was illegalized. That is the inseparable other half of the settler-colonial reality that is implicit in the Second Amendment. The first enslaved Africans to be shipped to Britain's first colony of the eventual thirteen colonies that became the United States took place in 1619, when twenty bonded Africans arrived in Virginia. Most of the labor being used in the first decade of the colony was made up of British and other Europeans who had indentured themselves for varying lengths of time, but African slavery was different. As Howard Zinn points out, "Some historians think those first blacks in Virginia were considered as servants, like the white indentured servants brought from Europe. But the strong probability is that, even if they were listed as 'servants' (a more familiar category to the English), they were viewed as being different from white servants, were treated differently, and in fact were slaves."[5]

Other scholars have presumed that the British settlers in North America were reluctant to enslave Africans, but that too seems a spurious notion. When the Doctrine of

Discovery promulgated by the Vatican in the mid-fifteenth century "legalized" the Portuguese capture and enslavement of the people of West Africa, the trans-Atlantic slave trade took off, first within European markets. Then, in 1492, it reached the Caribbean and had been in effect for over a century when the Virginia seaboard was wrenched from the Indigenous farmers by English usurpers. From the mid-fifteenth century to the mid-twentieth century, most of the non-European world was colonized under the Doctrine of Discovery, one of the first principles of international law promulgated by Christian European monarchies to legitimize investigating, mapping, and claiming lands belonging to peoples outside Europe. It originated in a papal bull issued in 1455 that permitted the Portuguese monarchy to seize West Africa for enslaving those who lived there. Following Columbus's infamous exploratory voyage in 1492, sponsored by the king and queen of the infant Spanish state, another papal bull extended similar permission to Spain. Disputes between the Portuguese and Spanish monarchies led to the papal-initiated Treaty of Tordesillas (1494), which, besides dividing the globe equally between the two Iberian empires, clarified that only non-Christian lands fell under the discovery doctrine.[6]

This doctrine, on which all European states relied, thus originated with the arbitrary and unilateral establishment of the Iberian monarchies' exclusive rights under Christian canon law to colonize, enslave, and exterminate foreign peoples, and these were later embraced by other European monarchical colonizing projects, such as the British in North America.

The only barrier to introducing slavery in Virginia and all the other colonies would have been economic, not ethical. The Southern colonies emerged in territory that had been one of seven original birthplaces of agriculture[7] in the world tens of thousands of years before, developed by the Muskogee and other Indigenous agricultural societies. Appropriated by European settlers, these lands would become economies based on enslaved African labor and increasingly on breeding enslaved people for profit, with the Indigenous farmers forced to the peripheries. At the time of U.S. independence, half the population of South Carolina was made up of enslaved Africans, with the other agribusiness colonies having large enslaved populations as well. By the late seventeenth century, onerous slave codes had been developed, which included mandatory slave patrols drawn from the already existing militias.

The wealthy slavers of the Southern colonies, particularly those in Virginia, were most incensed by the British Proclamation following the French and Indian War prohibiting expansion over the Appalachian ridge, since their wealth relied on accessing more and more land as they depleted the soils with intensive monocrop production for the market. They defied the Proclamation, taking survey teams into the Ohio country to map the territory for future settlement, which by definition meant the extension and expansion of slavery. By the time he was in his mid-twenties, George Washington was already a notoriously successful slaver and land speculator in unceded Indian lands.[8]

Washington and the other founders of the United States designed a governmental and economic structure to serve the private property interests of each and all of the primary actors, nearly all of them slavers and land speculators, with the brilliant Alexander Hamilton as the genius of finance. Like the Indian-killing militias that continued and intensified as the United States appropriated more land for slavers, slave patrols grew accordingly. The ethnic cleansing of Native Americans complete, slavers—with their reserve of capital and enslaved labor—transformed the Mississippi Valley into the Cotton Kingdom that formed the basis for U.S. capitalism and world trade. In the words of Harvard historian Walter Johnson, "The extension of slavery into the Mississippi Valley gave an institution that was in decline at the end of the eighteenth century new life in the nineteenth. In 1800, there were around 100,000 slaves living within the boundaries of the present-day states of Mississippi and Louisiana; in 1840, there were more than 250,000; in 1860, more than 750,000"[9]

The militaristic-capitalist powerhouse that the United States became by 1840 derived from real estate (which included enslaved Africans, as well as appropriated land). The United States was founded as a capitalist state and an empire on conquered land, with capital in the form of slaves, hence the term chattel slavery; this was exceptional in the world and has remained exceptional. The capitalist firearms industry was among the first successful modern corporations. Gun proliferation and gun violence today are among its legacies.

TWO

SAVAGE WAR

So, if ever built, what will the United States Native
American Genocide Memorial Museum contain:
What will it exhibit?
It will be one room, a fifty-foot square with the same
large photo filling the walls, ceiling, and floor.
There will only be one visitor allowed at any one time.
There will be no furniture.
That one visitor will have to stand or sit on the floor.
Or lie on the floor if they feel the need.
That visitor must remain in that room for one hour.
There will be no music
The only soundtrack will be random gunshots from
rifles used throughout American history.
Reverberation.
What will that one photo be?
It will be an Indian baby, shredded by a Gatling gun,
lying dead and bloody in the snow.

Sherman Alexie, from *You Don't Have*
to Say You Love Me[1]

The violence of settler colonialism stems from the use of "savage war" and is related to the militias of the Second Amendment. "Savage war"—also called *petite guerre* in military annals, and Anglo-America's "first way of war" by military historian John Grenier—dates to the British colonial period and is described as a combination of "unlimited war and irregular war," and a military tradition "that accepted, legitimized, and encouraged attacks upon and the destruction of noncombatants, villages and agricultural resources . . . in shockingly violent campaigns to achieve their goals of conquest."[2]

When compared to other countries that carried out colonial conquests in Africa, Asia, the Caribbean, and South America, the United States was not exceptional in the sheer amount of violence it imposed to achieve sovereignty over the territories it appropriated. The British colonizations of Canada, Australia, and New Zealand were equally genocidal. Extreme violence, particularly against unarmed families and communities, was an inherent aspect of European colonialism, always with genocidal possibilities, and often with genocidal results. What distinguishes the U.S. experience is not the amount or type of violence involved, but rather the historical narratives attached to that violence and their political uses, even today. From the first settlement, appropriating land from its stewards became a racialized war, "civilization" against "savagery," and thereby was inherently genocidal. In the words of historian Richard Slotkin, "'Savage war' was distinguished from 'civilized warfare' in its lack of limitations on the extent of violence, and of laws for its application. The doctrine of 'savage war' depended on the belief that certain races are inherently disposed to cruel and atrocious violence. Similar assumptions had often operated in the wars of Christian or crusading states against the Muslims in Europe and the Holy Land, and massacre had often enough accompanied such wars."[3]

Military historian John Grenier offers an indispensable analysis of the white colonists' warfare against the Indigenous peoples of North America. The way of war largely devised and enacted by settlers formed the basis for the founding ideology and colonialist military strategy of the independent United States, and this approach to war is still being practiced almost as a reflex in the twenty-first century.[4]

Grenier explains that he began his study after September 11, 2001, in the wake of the U.S. reversion to irregular warfare—savage warfare—in Afghanistan, then in Iraq, his goal to trace the historical roots of U.S. use of unlimited war as an attempt to destroy the collective will of enemy people, or their capacity to resist, employing any means necessary but mainly by attacking civilians and their support systems, such as their food supply. Today called "special operations" or "low-intensity conflict," that kind of warfare was first used against Indigenous communities by colonial militias in the first British colonies of Virginia and Massachusetts. Those irregular forces, made up of landed settlers, sought to disrupt every aspect of resistance as well as to obtain intelligence through scouting and taking prisoners. They did so by destroying Indigenous villages and fields and intimidating and slaughtering unarmed women, children, and elders.[5] These voluntary fighting crews made up of individual civilians—"rangers"—are the groups referenced as militias, as they came to be called, in the Second Amendment.

Grenier analyzes the development of the U.S. way of war from 1607 to 1814, during which all the architecture of the U.S. military was forged, leading to its extension and development into the present. Esteemed U.S. historian Bernard Bailyn labeled the period "barbarous," but Bailyn, like most of his fellow U.S. historians, portrays the Indigenous defenders of their homelands as "marauders" that the European settlers needed to get rid of.[6] From this formative period, Grenier argues, emerged problematic characteristics of the U.S. way of war and thereby the characteristics of its civilization, which few historians have come to terms with and many, such as Bailyn, justify as necessary.

During the late seventeenth century, Anglo settlers in New England began the routine practice of scalp hunting and "ranging." By that time, the non-Indigenous population of the British colony in North America had increased sixfold, to more than 150,000 people, which meant that settlers were intruding on more of the Indigenous farmlands and fishing resources. Indigenous resistance followed in what the settlers called "King Philip's War." Wampanoag people and their Indigenous allies attacked the settlers' isolated farms, using a method that relied on speed and caution in striking and retreating, and possessing of course a perfect knowledge of the terrain and climate.

The settlers scorned this kind of resistance as "skulking," and responded by destroying Indigenous villages and everyone in them who could not escape, burning their fields and food storage. But as effective Indigenous resistance continued, the commander of the Plymouth militia, Benjamin Church, studied Wampanoag tactics in order to develop a more effective kind of preemption or counterinsurgency. He petitioned the colony's governor for permission to choose sixty to seventy settlers to serve as scouts, as he called them, for what he termed "wilderness warfare," although they were attacking developed Indigenous villages and fields. In July 1676, the first settler-organized militia was the result. The rangers' force was made up of sixty male settlers and 140 already conquered Indigenous men. They were ordered to "discover, pursue, fight, surprise, destroy, or subdue" the enemy, in Church's words. The inclusion of Indigenous fighters on the colonists' side was not unique to British colonists in North America; rather, the practice has marked the character of European colonization and occupations of non-European peoples from the beginning. The settler-rangers could learn from their Native aides, then discard them. In the following two decades, Church perfected his evolving methods of annihilation, and those methods spread as more colonies were established.[7]

The Native people of New England continued to fight back by burning British settlements and killing settlers or capturing them for ransom. As an incentive to recruit fighters, colonial authorities introduced a program of scalp hunting that became a permanent and long-lasting element of settler warfare against Indigenous nations.[8] During the Pequot War, Connecticut and Massachusetts colonial officials had offered bounties initially for the heads of murdered Indigenous people and later for only their scalps, which were more portable in large numbers. But scalp hunting became routine and more profitable following an incident on the northern frontier of the Massachusetts colony. The practice began in earnest in 1697 when settler Hannah Duston, having murdered ten of her Abenaki captors in a nighttime escape, presented their ten scalps to the Massachusetts General Assembly and was rewarded with bounties for two men, two women, and six children.[9] However, it would be only in the 1820s that the Duston story was revived, and she was made famous as the first Euro American woman in North America to be celebrated with a statue. Duston was very famous for a few years after 1697, at the time of her escape from captivity, and her bloody scalp trophies were highly publicized at the time, but she had been pretty much forgotten until stories about her began to appear in print and increased in numbers through the 1880s. Not just one, but three major monuments were erected in her honor. Lionized as a folk hero, Duston and her story were employed during the continuing bloody and genocidal wars against Native peoples to characterize settler and Army violence as defensive and virtuous, necessary, even feminine.[10]

Scalp hunting became a lucrative commercial practice from the early eighteenth century onward. The settler authorities had hit upon a way to encourage settlers to take off on their own or with a few others to gather scalps, at random, for the reward money. "In the process," John Grenier points out, "they established the large-scale privatization of war within American frontier communities."[11]

In the beginning, Anglo settlers organized irregular units to brutally attack and destroy unarmed Indigenous women, children, and old people using unlimited violence in unrelenting attacks. During nearly two centuries of British colonization on the Atlantic shore of North America, generations of settlers gained experience as "Indian fight-ers" outside any organized military institution. The An-glo-French conflict may appear to have been the dominant factor of European colonization in North America during the eighteenth century, but while large regular armies fought over geopolitical goals in Europe, Anglo settlers in North America waged deadly irregular warfare against the Indigenous communities.

Much of the fighting during the eight-year settlers' war for independence, especially in the Ohio Valley region and western New York, was directed against Indigenous resisters who realized it was not in their interest to have a close enemy of Indian-hating settlers with their own independent gov-ernment, as opposed to a remote one in Great Britain with wider global interests. Nor did the fledgling U.S. military in the 1790s carry out operations typical of the state-centered wars occurring in Europe at the time. Even following the founding of the professional U.S. Army in the 1810s, irreg-ular warfare was the method used by the U.S. to conquer the Ohio Valley and Mississippi Valley regions. Since that time, Grenier notes, irregular methods have been used in tandem with operations of regular armed forces. The chief characteristic of irregular warfare is that of extreme violence against civilians, in this case the tendency to pursue the utter annihilation of the Indigenous population. "In cases where a rough balance of power existed," Grenier observes, "and the Indians even appeared dominant—as was the situation in virtually every frontier war until the first decade of the 19th century—[settler] Americans were quick to turn to extrava-gant violence."[12]

Many historians who acknowledge the exceptional one-sided colonial violence attribute it to racism. Grenier argues that rather than racism leading to violence, the reverse occurred: the out-of-control momentum of extreme violence of unlimited warfare fueled race hatred.

> Successive generations of Americans, both soldiers and civilians, made the killing of Indian men, women, and children a defining element of their first military tradition and thereby part of a shared American identity. Indeed, only after seventeenth- and early eighteenth-century Americans made the first way of war a key to being a white American could later generations of "Indian haters," men like Andrew Jackson, turn the Indian wars into race wars.[13]

By then, the Indigenous peoples' villages, farmlands, towns, and entire nations formed the only barrier to the settlers' total freedom to acquire land and wealth:

> U.S. people are taught that their military culture does not approve of or encourage targeting and killing civilians and know little or nothing about the nearly three centuries of warfare—before and after the founding of the U.S.—that reduced the Indigenous peoples of the continent to a few reservations by burning their towns and fields and killing civilians, driving the refugees out—step by step—across the continent. . . . [V]iolence directed systematically against noncombatants through

irregular means, from the start, has been a central part of Americans' way of war.[14]

Most military historians ignore the influence that the "Indian Wars," waged from 1607 to 1890, had on subsequent U.S. military operations. In his history of American "savage wars," *The Savage Wars of Peace: Small Wars and the Rise of American Power*, counterinsurgent war enthusiast Max Boot does not even mention the Indian Wars as being related to his thesis.[15] As Grenier notes, "Historians normally dismiss backcountry settlers' burning of Indian villages and fields as a sideshow to the Army's attempt to mold itself into a force like those found in Europe. Yet, the wars of the Upper Ohio Valley and on the Tennessee and western Georgia frontiers are vitally important to understanding the evolution of Americans' military heritage."[16]

Those wars are also vitally important to understanding one of the two rationales for the Second Amendment: The white settlers were clear in declaring that their intentions were to drive the Indians from lands on the western side of the mountain ranges and to claim those lands as their own. Andrew Jackson's career arc personifies this dance of settler militias and the professional army. Jackson was born in 1767 in a Scots-Irish community on the North Carolina border with South Carolina. His father died in an accident a short time before he was born. Raised poor by a single mother, at age thirteen Jackson became a courier for the local regiment of the frontier secessionists in their war of independence from Britain. Jackson's mother and brothers died during the war, leaving him an orphan with no family. He studied law and was admitted to the bar in the Western District of North Carolina, which would later become the state of Tennessee. Through his legal work, most of which related to disputed settler claims to Indian lands, he acquired a plantation near Nashville and enslaved 150 people for use as labor. He helped usher in Tennessee as a state in 1796. As the most notorious land speculator in western Tennessee, Jackson enriched himself by annexing a portion of the Chickasaw Nation's farmlands. It was in 1801 that Jackson first took command of the Tennessee militia as a colonel and began his ruthless Indian-killing military career, driving the Muskogee Nation out of Georgia. In the aftermath of "the Battle of Horseshoe Bend," as it is known in U.S. military annals, Jackson's troops fashioned reins for their horses' bridles from skin stripped from the Muskogee people they had killed, and they saw to it that souvenirs from the corpses were given "to the ladies of Tennessee." Following the slaughter, Jackson justified his troops' actions: "The fiends of the Tallapoosa will no longer murder our women and children, or disturb the quiet of our borders. . . . They have disappeared from the face of the Earth."[17]

In 1818, President James Monroe ordered Andrew Jackson, by then a major general in the U.S. Army, to lead three thousand soldiers into Florida, at the time part of the Spanish Empire, to crush the Muskogee-led Indigenous Seminole guerrilla resistance. The Seminoles did not agree to hand over any Africans who had escaped from their white enslavers. The United States annexed Florida as a territory in 1819, opening it to settlement. In 1821 Jackson was appointed military commander of Florida Territory.

Jackson carried out the original plan envisioned by the founders—particularly Jefferson—initially as a militia leader, then as an army general who led four wars of aggression against the Muskogee Creek and Seminoles in Georgia and Florida, and finally as a president who engineered the forced expulsion of all Native peoples east of the Mississippi to the designated "Indian Territory." As historian Alan Brinkley has observed, Jackson's political fortunes depended on the fate of the Indians—that is, their eradication.

Richard Slotkin describes a mystique that developed around the persona of the ranger, involving a certain identification with the Native enemy, marking the settler as original American rather than European. "By dressing and fighting as Indians, the ranger appropriated the savage's power and American nativity for himself and turned it against both savage and redcoat."[18] Following independence, this mystique became a part of popular culture, as well as military culture.

The formation of the Texas Rangers to extinguish Native presence in Texas after Southern slavers took it from Mexico magnified their mystique. Following the independence of Mexico from Spain in 1821, the territory of Mexico comprised the provinces of California, New Mexico (including Arizona and Colorado), and Texas, even though much of that territory was never actually settled by the Spanish, particularly the huge province of Texas. Mexico established "colonization" laws that allowed non-Mexican citizens to acquire large swaths of land under land grants that required development, and implied eradication of the resident Native people. By 1836, nearly forty thousand U.S. Americans, almost all of them Cotton Kingdom slavers, had moved to south Texas. Their ranger militias were a part of the settlement, and in 1835 were formally institutionalized as the Texas Rangers. Once they were state funded and sponsored, they were tasked with eradicating the Comanche nation and all other Native peoples from Texas, what historian Gary Clayton Anderson calls the "ethnic cleansing of Texas."[19] Mounted and armed with the newest killing machine, the five-shot Colt Paterson revolver, they used it with dedicated precision.

While continuing violent counterinsurgency operations against Comanches and other Indigenous communities, the Texas Rangers played a significant role in the U.S. invasion of Mexico in 1846–48. As seasoned counterinsurgents, they guided U.S. Army forces deep into Mexico, engaging in the battle of Monterrey. Rangers accompanied General Winfield Scott's army by sea; took part in the siege of Veracruz, Mexico's main commercial port city; then marched on, leaving a path of corpses and destruction to occupy Mexico City, where the citizens called them Texas Devils, as the Rangers roamed the city terrorizing civilian residents. Brutalized by yet another foreign power, Mexico ceded the northern half of its territory (including the illegally Anglo-occupied Texas) to the United States. Texas became a state of the United States in 1845, seceding to join the Confederacy in 1860. The Texas Rangers returned to warring on Native communities and harassing resistant Mexicans.

During the second half of the nineteenth century, the Army of the West continued to combat the peoples of the Southwest and of the Northern Plains to the Pacific, formerly a part of Mexico. Military analyst Robert Kaplan challenges the concept of Manifest Destiny, arguing "it was not inevitable that the United States should have an empire in the western part of the continent." Rather, he argues, Western empire was brought about by "small groups of frontiersmen, separated from each other by great distances." These groups were the continuation of settler "rangers" that destroyed Indigenous towns, fields, and food supplies. Kaplan downplays the role of the U.S. Army compared to the settler vigilantes, which he equates to modern Special Forces, but he acknowledges that the regular army provided lethal backup for settler counterinsurgency in slaughtering the buffalo, thus disrupting the food supply of Plains peoples, as well as making continuous raids on settlements to kill or confine the families of the Indigenous fighters. Kaplan summarizes the genealogy of U.S. militarism today: "Whereas the average American at the dawn of the new millennium found patriotic inspiration in the legacies of the Civil War and World War II, when the evils of slavery and fascism were confronted and vanquished, for many commissioned and noncommissioned officers the U.S. Army's defining moment was fighting the 'Indians.'"[20]

Although the U.S. Constitution formally instituted "militias" as state-controlled bodies that were subsequently deployed to wage wars against Native Americans, the voluntary militias described in the Second Amendment entitled settlers, as individuals and families, to the right to combat Native Americans on their own. However, savage war was also embedded in the U.S. Marines, established at independence, as well as the Special Forces of the Army and Navy, established in the mid-twentieth century. The Marine

Corps was founded in 1775, a year after the thirteen colonies formed the Continental Congress and Army, a year before the Declaration of Independence, thirteen years before the U.S. Constitution was ratified forming the state, and twenty-three years before the U.S. Navy was founded. The following year, the Marines made their first landing, capturing an island in the Bahamas from the British, what in Marine Corps history is called "Fort Nassau." In action throughout the Revolutionary War, the Marines were disbanded in 1783 and reorganized in 1794 as a branch of the United States Navy.

The character of a Marine is that of the colonial ranger, created for counterinsurgency outside U.S.-secured territory. The opening lyric of the eternal official hymn of the U.S. Marine Corps, composed and adopted in 1847, soon after the invasion of Mexico and during the occupation, is "From the Halls of Montezuma to the shores of Tripoli." Tripoli hearkens back nearly a half century to the "Barbary Wars" of 1801–15, when the Marines were dispatched to North Africa by President Thomas Jefferson to invade the Berber Nation, continuing this aggression, shelling the city, taking captives, and marauding for nearly four years, ending with the 1805 "Battle of Derna." It was there they earned the nickname "leathernecks" for the high collars they wore as defense against the Berbers' saber cuts. This was the "First Barbary War," the ostensible goal of which was to persuade Tripoli to release U.S. sailors it held hostage and to end what the U.S. called "pirate" attacks on U.S. merchant ships. Actually, the Berbers were demanding that their sovereignty over their territorial waters be respected. The Berbers did not give up their demands, and the Marines were withdrawn, returning a decade later, in 1815–16, for the "Second Barbary War," which ended when Pasha Yusuf Karamanli, ruler of Tripoli, agreed not to exact fees from U.S. ships entering their territorial waters. This was the first military victory of U.S. "gunboat diplomacy," as it came to be called nearly a century later, when historians mark the beginning of U.S overseas imperialism. The Marines and military historians know better.

The Marine Corps's second large engagement was the Second Seminole War, which raged from 1835 to 1842 in Florida, the longest war in U.S. history until Vietnam. The Second Seminole War during the Jackson administration has been identified with the extraordinary leader of the Seminole resistance, Osceola. It was all-out war with the Army, Navy, and Marine Corps involved. Although, they succeeded in killing Osceola, they lost the war as the Seminoles would not hand over the Africans who had escaped their slavers, which is what the United States demanded of them. The military did succeed in deporting captives, mostly women, children, and old men, to Indian Territory. Armed forces returned to try again in 1855, waging the Third Seminole War, but after four years of siege, lost again. Soon after, the Civil War and the abolition of slavery made further war against the Seminoles unnecessary.

Of course, the Marine Corps is associated with "the halls of Montezuma," lyrics from their trademark hymn composed while they occupied Mexico City in 1847. While the U.S. Army invaded and occupied what is now California, Arizona, and New Mexico, the Marines invaded by sea and occupied Veracruz, using counterinsurgency tactics in their march to Mexico City, burning fields and villages, murdering and torturing civilian resisters. They occupied Mexico City, along with Army divisions, until the Mexican government, under brutal occupation, signed a dubious treaty transferring the northern half of Mexico to the United States. In Marine Corps annals, the 1847 "Battle of Chapultepec" is legion, a battle in which a handful of teenage Mexican cadets—the Chapultepec Castle was used as a military training school—with few weapons and little ammunition held off the Marines, killing most of them over two days of endless fighting in the castle, until the cadets themselves were dead and the remaining Marines raised the U.S. flag and wrote their hymn, tracing their genealogy to the invasion and occupation of Tripoli.

In a 2017 portrait of President Donald Trump's secretary of defense, retired Marine Corps general James "Mad Dog" Mattis, journalist Dexter Filkins writes that Marines see themselves as a kind of warrior caste with "toughness under fire, and savagery in battle. Being much smaller than the Army, its budgets are skimpier and the equipment sometimes antiquated, while its fighters are often pitched into terrible conditions. But, the Marines take their scant resources as a source of pride. Where the Army scatters recruits across a vast institution that includes accountants and mechanics who have little contact with the harsher realities of military work, every Marine is trained as a rifleman, a combatant."[21]

Later in the century, Marine actions, particularly the infamous war in the Philippines, and others up to the present, are well known, but they themselves take pride in their origins, which most U.S. Americans, including leftists, know little or nothing about. If they did, they would have to reconsider the overlooked violence in the nation's founding narratives.

The United States is a militarized culture. We see it all around us and in the media. But, as military historian John Grenier notes, the cultural aspects of militarization are not new; they have deep historical roots, reaching into the nation's racist settler past and continuing through unrelenting wars of conquest and ethnic cleansing over three centuries. Grenier writes, "Beyond its sheer military utility, Americans also found a use for the first way of war in the construction of an 'American identity.' . . . [T]he enduring appeal of the romanticized myth of the 'settlement' (not calling it conquest) of the frontier, either by 'actual' men such as Robert Rogers or Daniel Boone or fictitious ones like Nathaniel Bumppo of James Fenimore Cooper's creation, points to what D.H. Lawrence called the 'myth of the essential white American.'"[22]

The astronomical number of firearms owned by U.S. civilians, with the Second Amendment considered a sacred mandate, is also intricately related to militaristic culture and white nationalism. The militias referred to in the Second Amendment were intended as a means for white people to eliminate Indigenous communities in order to take their land, and for slave patrols to control Black people.

THREE

SLAVE PATROLS

Following the Rodney King riots in Los Angeles and the development of Cop Watch groups in cities around the United States, along with the widespread incarceration of Black men in the 1990s,[1] what had long been known by scholars, but rarely acknowledged in media or history texts, became increasingly clear on a national level: The origins of policing in the United States were rooted in slave patrols.[2]

In a study of slave patrols in Virginia and the Carolinas in 1700–1865, historian and law professor Sally E. Hadden writes: "People other than masters or overseers had legitimate rights, indeed, legal duties, to regulate slave behavior."[3] Black people escaping to freedom were hunted down to prevent labor loss to their white slavers, and also to send a message to those enslaved who might be strategizing to lose their chains through rebellion or insurrection.

Because chattel slavery was uncommon in the 1500s in England itself, the existing legal system that colonists brought to the early British colonies in North America did not suffice, so nearly all law related to slavery was forged in the colonies, borrowing from existing practices in Spanish, Portuguese, and English Caribbean plantation colonies, and specifically borrowing the use of slave patrols from the Caribbean and adapting them to local conditions on the continent.

The 1661 and 1688 slave codes in the British Caribbean colony of Barbados extended the task of controlling enslaved Africans from overseers and slavers to all white settlers, in effect shifting private responsibility to the public. Any enslaved person outside the direct control of the slaver or overseer required passes and was subject to questioning by a slave patrol, as well as by any member of the European population; free Black men were denied such power. This collective racial policing was in addition to the traditional English constabulary that investigated and detained European residents for infractions of laws.

British slavers from Barbados moved in large numbers to the South Carolina colony after 1670, and brought the slave patrol practice with them.[4] By 1704, the South Carolina colonial government had codified slave patrols and embedded them within the already existing volunteer militias, whose principal role was to repel Native Americans whose land they had appropriated. Members of slave patrols were drawn from militia rolls in every locale. The South Carolina structure of slave patrols was adopted in other colonies by the mid-eighteenth century and would remain relatively unchanged until the Civil War. Following U.S. independence, this structure and practice was applied to what became the Cotton Kingdom, following the U.S. wars against the Muskogee peoples that ended in their forced relocation to Indian Territory.[5]

Virginia was the first of the thirteen English settler

colonies in North America, but there were fewer enslaved Africans there, and they were more widely dispersed than in South Carolina, as Virginia settlements were long surrounded by resistant Native communities. The Virginia militia was founded for one purpose: to kill Indians, take their land, drive them out, wipe them out. European settlers were required by law to own and carry firearms, and all adult male settlers were required to serve in the militia. Militias were also used to prevent indentured European servants from fleeing before their contracts expired, in which case they were designated "debtors." Despite militia vigilance, many escaped on ships in ports

During the 1660s and 1670s, Virginia settlers turned from indenturing Europeans to importing enslaved Africans, and by 1680, the enslaved were required to carry passes. Of course, slave uprisings increased, and in 1705, the Virginia colony enacted its first slave code and established slave patrols. Militia members, focused on attacking Indigenous towns and fields to expand the Virginia colony refused to participate in slave patrols, so the colonial authorities imposed harsh punishments to control the enslaved Africans, such as death for even mentioning rebellion. Colonists prohibited the enslaved Africans from holding meetings or learning how to read. In 1727, the Virginia colony enacted a law requiring militias to create slave patrols, imposing stiff fines on white people who refused to serve.[6]

After 1650, slavers in Virginia began expanding deeper into the territory of the Tuscarora Nation, and were the first English settlers in what became the North Carolina colony in 1729. During the first three decades of Virginia settler incursion, the colony's militia was used solely to attack and burn down Tuscarora towns, incinerate their crops, and slaughter the families who resided there. By 1722, the embattled Tuscaroras joined the Haudenosaunee (Iroquois Confederacy) and migrated north for protection from settler terrorism, while some communities remained in severely deteriorating conditions.

In 1715, North Carolina's slaver government began requiring passes for enslaved individuals who were in public spaces doing errands or rented out as craftsmen, as many were escaping from bondage to Spanish Florida or marooning in the swamps of Cape Fear. Militias were used for pursuing Africans escaping to freedom, but did not form specific slave patrols as a separate category. In 1753, fearing increasing slave rebellions, the North Carolina colony established what they called "searchers," not drawn from the militias but authorized by courts; later they would be called "patrollers." They were exempt from militia duty as well as from jury duty and taxation, and two decades later, actually were paid salaries.[7]

Public patrols of varying types were established in all the slave colonies, but, significantly, any individual, including free Blacks or Natives, could claim a reward for capturing a person escaping from slavery, a practice that continued until the end of the Civil War. If weapons were found with the captive, the catcher could collect compensation for the weapons or keep them.[8]

After Independence, rapid expansion of slavery into newly conquered Native territories brought a concurrent increase in slave patrols, but the basic structure remained.

An 1860 judicial hornbook, *The Practice at Law in North Carolina* is an example:

> The patrol shall visit the negro houses in their respective districts as often as may be necessary, and may inflict a punishment, not exceeding fifteen lashes, on all slaves they may find off their owner's plantations, without a proper permit or pass, designating the place or places, to which the slaves have leave to go. The patrol shall also visit all suspected places, and suppress all unlawful collections of slaves; shall be diligent in apprehending all runaway negroes in their respective districts; shall be vigilant and endeavor to detect all thefts, and bring the perpetrators to justice, and also all persons guilty of trading with slaves; and if, upon taking up a slave and chastising him, as herein directed, he shall behave insolently, they may inflict further punishment for his misconduct, not exceeding thirty-nine lashes.[9]

In *Slave Patrols*, historian Hadden argues that the notion that slave patrols were made up of impoverished white men,[10] as portrayed in *Gone with the Wind* and *Uncle Tom's Cabin*, is false. She cautions against conflating entrepreneurial individual "slave catchers" and slave patrollers. Whether rich or poor, all Euro American males were required to serve in militias and slave patrols, but the commanders of the patrols were property owners and slavers. Impoverished whites were not trusted and would be unable to compensate a slaver for the property loss entailed in a death or injury incurred during an attempted capture.[11]

Writing about slavery in the Cotton Kingdom during the decades before the Civil War, historian Walter Johnson points to the central role horses played in subjugating runaways. Horses were a symbol of power for slavers, not only for show and racing, but as a physical symbol of racial power. "The words 'slave patrol' summon to mind a vision of white men on horseback, an association so definitive that it elides the remarkable fact that the geographic pattern of county governance in the South emerged out of circuits ridden by eighteenth-century slave patrols."[12] It was not only the advantage of height and speed that a horse provided in pursuing a person on the run, but also the nature of the animal itself, its own power, the fear the huge, galloping animal could evoke, and the severe bodily harm it inflicted when it trampled a person or when the patroller tethered a bound captive to the horse.

Another tool was the widely distributed "wanted" flier that alerted the public to be on the lookout, which attracted Euro Americans from hundreds of miles away to hunt freedom-seekers for bounty. And of course, slavers used dogs. Resistant Africans marooned in the swamps, or if fleeing rested there, where horses could not travel and most settlers were afraid to enter. Bloodhounds were trained from pups to identify and hunt Black people. "'Loyal' to their masters (or those to whom their masters hired them) and able to travel more rapidly than any human being across even the most difficult ground, these weaponized dogs were implacable enemies, driven by a purpose beyond that of even their owners."[13]

And above all, there were the guns. Historians Ned Sublette and Constance Sublette write:

> Unlike England, Virginia was a gun culture. "Whereas in England, only men with estates valued at above one hundred pounds sterling were allowed to own guns," writes Kathleen M. Brown, "English men in Virginia at all levels of property ownership were *expected* to own them. . . ." Guns and slavery were intimately associated with each other; all slave-raiding relied on guns, and all slaveholding relied on armed repression.[14]

By the early 1820s, slave-worked plantation agribusiness in Tidewater Virginia waned as the soils were degraded from mono-production and over-production, and investments moved to the Mississippi Valley. Nevertheless, slave patrols actually increased in Virginia, where the main commercial "crop" of the plantations was the enslaved person's body, as farms turned into breeding factories to produce slaves to be sold in the Cotton Kingdom.[15] Thomas Jefferson bragged to George Washington that the birth of Black children was increasing Virginia's capital stock by 4 percent annually. It is estimated that in 1860 the total value of enslaved African bodies in the United States was $4 billion, far more than the gold and silver then circulating nationally ($228.3 million, "most of it in the North," the authors add), total currency ($435.4 million), and even the value of the South's total farmland ($1.92 billion).[16]

Like slave patrols in the Deep South, the Texas

Rangers—formed primarily to kill Comanches, eliminate
Native communities, and control colonized Mexicans to
take their land—also hunted down enslaved Africans escaping to freedom. They began to operate in the 1820s, even
before the population of slavers in the independent province
of Texas had seceded from Mexico in 1836, when Mexico
formally outlawed slavery. With the new border in place,
enslaved Africans in Texas could escape into Mexico, often
with the help of armed Seminoles and Kickapoos, who had
fled to take refuge in Mexico rather than remain in Indian
Territory, where they had been forced to migrate when the
United States annexed their lands east of the Mississippi.
They created a community west of Piedras Negras far inside
Mexico, and a place for them to live freely. When the United States Army and Marines invaded and occupied Mexico,
departing only when Mexico had ceded half its territory to
the United States, these maroon communities were vulnerable. Slave hunting escalated, by the Rangers as well as by
individual bounty hunters.[17]

The Thirteenth Amendment abolished legal chattel
slavery, but the surveillance of Black people by patrols continued, as the occupying Union army took no concerted action against the patrols in most places (depending on the
army commander), forcing formerly enslaved Africans to
remain and work on plantations. Even with military vigilance, "patrolling" Black people continued as a form of organized terrorism, perpetrated especially by the Ku Klux
Klan, which was founded for that very purpose nineteen
months after the Civil War ended. The intensive military
training and experience over four years of fighting in the

Confederate Army produced a militaristic character to the formation of police forces and patrol techniques under Reconstruction; in addition, the Freedmen no longer even had the protection of being valued as property and collateral by former slavers, allowing for extreme forms of revenge violence against them.[18]

When Republicans were elected to state offices, they attempted to reform local militias requiring all males to serve, regardless of race, but few Anglo-Americans would serve with Freedmen. Freedmen did serve in the state militias, but they also developed their own local volunteer militia groups. Former slavers spread rumors that Freedmen were forming insurrectionary armies to kill white people. White elites formed agricultural cooperatives to maintain economic dominance over Freedmen, a goal one group made clear: "a united and systematic plan with respect to the regulation of our colored population."[19] They also created their own forces to intimidate other Anglo-American farmers and merchants who attempted to trade with Black farmers, often putting white merchants out of business.

Most ominously, elite white Southerners formed volunteer militias under the guise of private rifle clubs. By 1876, South Carolina had more than 240 such clubs. This allowed thousands of Confederate combat veterans, along with former Confederate guerrillas, to mobilize quickly. Of course, the KKK was the most ominous terrorist organization to emerge from these efforts, its purpose being to subdue the Freedmen and control black labor when slavery ended. But the KKK was not alone. Either by their absence in many places or their actions in others, some of the U.S. Army officers in charge made these developments possible. One that stands out is U.S. General E.R.S. Canby, a Kentuckian who was occupation commander of the Carolinas. Canby refused to make use of his own soldiers, and instead relied on white Southern law enforcement to maintain order. He had to have known what would happen. Like many U.S. Civil War commanders assigned to the occupation army of the former Confederacy, in 1872 he soon reassigned to the Army of the West, where he commanded troops to round up several dozen Modoc families in Northern California who refused to be forced into an Oregon reservation. The Modocs waged a year-long resistance to the Army's counterinsurgency, finally killing General Canby.[20] One of the reasons troops were pulled out of the South prematurely was to fight in the dozens of wars the United States was initiating against Indigenous Nations in the Northern Plains, the Southwest, and the West.[21]

As Hadden points out, Southern settlers had long relied on "self-help" measures to enforce slavery leading up to the formalized slave patrols, which had continued where possible during the Civil War. What was different after the abolition of slavery was the tons of technologically advanced guns and ammunition, and the tens of thousands of militarily seasoned and violent men who made ideal candidates for the Klan. Particularly, when the Confederate war hero Nathan Bedford Forrest joined the Klan, it gained a chivalric image that attracted other war heroes. Congress enacted laws forbidding secret groups, but the laws were rarely enforced.[22]

In fact, the United States never broke with the slaveocracy, as exemplified in the career of Nathan Bedford Forrest. He lost his parents and economic security at seventeen, but became a slave trader, land speculator, and finally a wealthy slaver with his own large plantation. He was the epitome of the "self-made" man that was the vaunted ideal of white supremacy. In the Civil War, Forrest was a cavalry officer for the Confederate Army, infamous for having led the massacre of hundreds of Black Union soldiers in 1864, a war crime. Yet President Andrew Johnson granted Forrest a presidential pardon in 1868.[23]

The Klan, illegal as it was, operated like a huge slave patrol, requiring Freedmen to have written permission to travel from the plantations where many continued to work. The Klan established curfews for gatherings of African Americans, as well as limits on the number who could gather. The Klan burned homes, confiscated the guns of Freedmen, and, of course, inflicted punishment similar to slave patrols' beatings, but also had far more freedom to torture and murder, since the Black body no longer carried monetary value that the murderer would have to compensate for. Of course, Black people resisted, as they had resisted the slave patrols. However, the Klan was a private terrorist organization, not a public force, and had no legal status or accountability. Some Klansmen were put on trial, but none was ever convicted. Occasionally, the U.S. Army would declare martial law, but as one army commander said in 1871, "The entire United States Army would be insufficient to give protection throughout the South to everyone in possible danger from the Klan."[24]

From the perspective of African Americans who survived the organized violence, there was no distinction between patrollers, Klan, and white policemen, whether rural, in towns, or in the cities. In nineteenth-century criminal digests, arrests made by slave patrollers before the Civil War continued to be used as legal precedents in the 1880s.

Hadden notes that the language of slave patrols is still employed in police work in the twenty-first century, "patrol" being the most obvious, but also "beat." More disturbingly, techniques were folded into police practices, such as surveillance methods like the stakeout. And until the 1960s pushback, police had little supervision and routinely brutalized and confined suspects without consequences; even in the twenty-first century, when police torture or murder Black people, juries rarely find the involved officers guilty of any crime.[25]

In the first four decades of the twentieth century, around 6 million African Americans left the South. With World War II, 1.5 million more left the South between 1940 and 1950, many to work in the war industry in California. More than 300,000 Black Southerners migrated to the greater Los Angeles and San Francisco Bay areas during that decade. And, during the Depression and droughts of the 1930s, a wave of some 400,000 mostly Anglo Oklahomans, Texans, Arkansans, and Missourians poured into California, followed by another wave to work in the war industry in the 1940s.

In 1950, William Parker became chief of the Los Angeles Police Department (LAPD) for the following decade and a half, ending after the 1965 Watts Uprising. The LAPD was already virtually all white and solidly racist, with mainly Mexicans making up the oppressed and controlled target community. With the goal of controlling the increasing African American blue-collar population in South Central Los

Angeles, Parker began recruiting Anglo veterans from the South and Southwest who had settled in Southern California after the Dust Bowl migrations or military service. The new technology of television brought the series *Dragnet* to homes all over the country, extolling the LAPD and attracting recruits, as well as influencing other urban police forces all over the country. During this time, the LAPD became the most notorious racist police operation ("police culture") in the country, with nearly every aspect of the Southern tradition of slave patrols woven into the system.[26] A similar police force was formed in Oakland, where many Black veterans and war-industry workers had settled. At the same time, the Civil Rights movement was making widespread gains, with school integration mandated by law and growing Black resistance to police violence in the South, in Northern cities, and in Los Angeles and Oakland.

In an article for *The Atlantic*, liberal writers Saul Cornell and Eric M. Ruben make a strong argument for the slave-state origins of modern gun rights. Certainly, any inquiry into the institutionalization of slave patrols in those colonies/states reveals the connection with the Second Amendment.[27] However, this does not explain why the N.R.A. and gun rights are so popular in other parts of the country. Armed slave patrols comprise half the story in the Second Amendment; the whole story implicates more than the slave states. While the "savage wars" against Native Nations instituted brutal modes of violence for the U.S. military, and slave patrols seamlessly evolved into modern police forces, both have normalized racialized violence and affinity for firearms in U.S. society.

FOUR

CONFEDERATE GUERRILLAS TO OUTLAW ICONS

I grew up in rural Oklahoma. Both my parents were born in western Missouri. My father, besides being a tenant farmer and rodeo man, was an actual proletarian cowboy who worked on a large cattle ranch in Oklahoma mending fences and herding cattle long distances before he married my mother. In this world, stories of "Robin Hood" outlaw heroes were pervasive. These included the James Gang, Jesse and Frank; the Younger Brothers, Cole, Jim, John, and Bob; and Belle Starr—dubbed the "Bandit Queen"— my female role model. I was, thanks to my mother, a devout Southern Baptist, yet it didn't seem contradictory that these bandits broke nearly all the Ten Commandments, because they stole from the rich and gave to the poor, or so it was said. Not until I moved to San Francisco when I was twenty-one and took a college course in U.S. West History did I learn that all my heroes had been Confederate guerrillas associated with William Quantrill's Rangers. They all came from middle-class families who bought, sold, and worked enslaved Africans, and who were devoted to the Confederacy, that is, the preservation of chattel slavery. This came as a shock, because I had for the previous four years taken sides in favor of the Civil Rights movement and despised racism, the main reason I left Oklahoma as soon as I could. I've been trying to figure out this disconnect ever since. But I do know that border-outlaw narratives have played a role in gun fetishism and a culture of violence in the United States.

I was not alone in buying into the myths about these outlaws. Even in San Francisco, New York City, and beyond, during the folk music revival of the late 1950s, Woody Guthrie's 1939 recording of the 1882 traditional song extolling Jesse James was revived and made the pop charts:[1]

> *Oh, they laid poor Jesse in his grave, yes, Lord*
> *They laid Jesse James in his grave*
> *Oh, he took from the rich and he gave to the poor*
> *But they laid Jesse James in his grave*

Pete Seeger recorded the song in 1957, followed by Eddy Arnold in 1959, the Kingston Trio in 1961, and in the 1970s it made the charts again, recorded by the Nitty Gritty Dirt Band as well as by Bob Seger; even The Pogues and Bruce Springsteen got into the act in the mid-1980s. It was recorded by dozens of other lesser-known folk, pop, and country musicians.

And there was a larger theme of sympathy for the slave South's "Lost Cause" in the 1960s counterculture. The Band first recorded "The Night They Drove Old Dixie Down," with lyrics by Robbie Robertson,[2] in 1969, when they were closely associated with Bob Dylan, topping the charts in several categories; Joan Baez recorded it in 1971, with the same result, as did Johnny Cash in 1975. Liberal San Francisco music critic Ralph J. Gleason waxed eloquent on The Band's recording: "Nothing I have read . . . has brought home the overwhelming human sense of history that this song does. . . . It's a remarkable song, the rhythmic structure, the voice of Levon [Helms] and the bass line with the drum accents and then the heavy close harmony of Levon, Richard and Rick in the theme, make it seem impossible that this isn't some traditional material handed down from father to son straight from that winter of 1865 to today. It has that ring of truth and the whole aura of authenticity."[3]

> *Virgil Kane is the name . . .*
> *In the winter of '65, we were hungry, just barely alive*
> *By May the tenth, Richmond had fell, it's a time I*
> *   remember, oh so well*
> *The night they drove old Dixie down, and the bells were*
> *   ringing . . .*
> *Ya take what ya need and ya leave the rest,*
> *But they should never have taken the very best . . .*
> *Like my father before me, I will work the land*
> *Like my brother above me, who took a rebel stand*
> *He was just eighteen, proud and brave, but a Yankee laid*
> *   him in his grave*

This was a post–World War II composition mourning the Confederate defeat in the Civil War, written by Robbie Robertson, also a member of The Band and one of the most celebrated of the many musicians, writers, and producers coming out of the 1960s. He is also Mohawk, his mother from the Six Nations Reserve outside Toronto, Canada, his father Jewish. Not having grown up in the United States, Robertson likely had very little knowledge of the Civil War, but Joan Baez did and was a pacifist and an icon of the African American Civil Rights movement of the time. It seems that the sanitized lore that views bloody, murdering, Confederate guerrillas as righteous outlaws continues to be deeply engrained in United States culture.[4]

It wasn't just the music counterculture, but also mainstream pop culture. *True Grit*, a best-selling 1968 novel by Charles Portis, also serialized in the popular mass-distributed magazine *The Saturday Evening Post*, was made into a blockbuster movie in 1969, featuring John Wayne as the fictional Rooster Cogburn, former Confederate guerrilla with Quantrill. John Wayne won the Academy Award for best acting in the role of the good-hearted drunken anti-hero who proves himself a true hero. Ethan and Joel Coen did a 2010 remake of the film for the new generation starring Jeff Bridges in the John Wayne role, accompanied by a new edition of the novel with an afterword by best-selling author Donna Tartt, which reached number one on the *New York Times* best-seller list.

The 1976 film *The Outlaw Josey Wales*, directed by Clint Eastwood and scripted by Forrest Carter, adapting his 1972 novel *The Rebel Outlaw: Josey Wales*, featured a Missouri Confederate guerrilla played by Clint Eastwood and was based on the true story of Bill Wilson, a folk hero in the Ozarks. After Union troops murder his wife and child, Wales refuses to surrender at the end of the war, seeks revenge, and guns down the Union man who murdered his family. He then flees to Texas with a bounty on his head. In the film, Josey Wales expresses his worldview: "Now remember, things look bad and it looks like you're not gonna make it, then you gotta get mean. I mean plumb, mad-dog mean. Cause if you lose your head and give up then you neither live nor win. That's just the way it is."[5]

Forrest Carter, who wrote the script for *The Outlaw Josey Wales*, is the pen name of Asa Earl Carter (1925–1979) who was a leader in the Ku Klux Klan in the 1950s and a speechwriter for the segregationist Alabama governor George Wallace in the 1960s. He changed his name and successfully turned to writing, first the Josey Wales book, then in 1976 what claimed to be a memoir, *The Education of Little Tree*.[6] The story is told by an orphaned boy of five years old, being raised by Cherokee grandparents who called him "Little Tree," with stereotypical noble savage actions and settings, perfect for the growing "New Age" appropriation and distortion of Native ways. At the book's release, *The New York Times* published an article outing Forrest Carter as Asa Carter, former Klansman. It was not a big secret, as Carter had run for governor of Alabama in 1970. The article reported, "Beyond denying that he is Asa Carter, the author has declined to be interviewed on the subject."[7]

Carter died at age 53 in 1979, beaten to death in a fight with his son. His literary fame faded. There had been no questioning of Carter's claim of Cherokee identity until the University of New Mexico Press bought the rights to *The Education of Little Tree* in 1985, and published it as nonfiction in 1991. The book took off and became the number one best seller on the *New York Times* best-seller list, won the American Booksellers Book of the Year award, and became a much loved book. The Cherokee Nation denied that Carter was Cherokee, and Carter's Ku Klux Klan background was once again revealed, leading the *Times* to shift the book to its fiction list. Despite calls from the Native American academic community and the Cherokee Nation that the University of New Mexico Press withdraw the book from publication, instead they changed the cover, removing the "True Story" subtitle, and reclassified it as fiction, but the biographical profile did not change to include Carter's Klan activities and the lack of evidence of his being Cherokee; it remains one of their best-selling books. Oprah Winfrey had endorsed the book when it was published, but removed it from her recommendations in 1994.

Clint Eastwood, directing *The Outlaw Josey Wales*, featured several stereotypical Native American characters, written by Carter and performed by excellent Native American actors, Geraldine Keams as a love interest, the elderly Chief Dan George as the protagonist's spirit guide, and Will Sampson as a protector. In the script, there is no mention of slavery, even though Wales was a Confederate guerrilla who rejected the Confederate defeat.

Two other widely viewed films—*Bonnie and Clyde* and *Pat Garret and Billy the Kid*—glorified the gun violence of real-life outlaws who were not Confederate guerrillas, but have contributed to those narratives being folded into ones of the Wild West, even though Bonnie and Clyde were bandits in the Great Depression era and Billie the Kid's short life ended in 1882. With *Bonnie and Clyde*, Arthur Penn broke through to mainstream box-office triumph and was embraced by the counterculture of 1967 at the same time. The film was noted for the bloodiest scenes in film history, and starred Warren Beatty and Faye Dunaway. Sam Peckinpah's 1973 film *Pat Garret and Billy the Kid* featured the popular musician and songwriter Kris Kristofferson as the Kid and a memorable soundtrack by Bob Dylan, who also played a cameo role.

How did it happen that popular culture transformed Confederate guerrillas into celebrity Western gunfighters, merging them with actual Western gunfighters, and what has this phenomenon contributed to the culture of violence and gun-love in the United States?

As explored in the previous two chapters, Euro American settlers had a long tradition of organized violence against unarmed civilian populations, their habitats, and their food supplies, beginning with the first early seventeenth-century incursions into Indigenous communities that reached global proportions in the "French and Indian War" (the North American theater of the 1754–1763 Seven Years' War between England and France), which was fought over colonialist domination of Native territories, followed soon after by the Anglo settlers' violent eight-year war for independence from Britain. In the first half of the nineteenth century, U.S. Americans' counterinsurgent operations and wars continued against resistant Natives, Mexicans, Mormons, and, in the Missouri-Kansas border conflict over slavery of the 1850s, each other, continuing through the Civil War itself. In dealing with the Civil War specifically, historians often divide guerrilla combatants into a top-down hierarchy, distinguishing between cavalry raiders, partisan rangers, and bushwhackers, the latter low category reserved for the Missouri-Kansas guerrillas. Guerrillas of these three types were part of the total war strategies of both the Union and Confederate armies, but in the case of the Missouri-border bushwhackers, they were outside any command structure and lacking actual battlefields in Missouri. These were small volunteer units under a leader the most famous being William Clarke Quantrill and "Bloody" Bill Anderson that attacked any sign of Union presence or suspected sympathies with the Union. This included an early morning assault on pro-Union Lawrence, Kansas, in which more than two hundred residents were massacred. During the Civil War, these bands were continuing a decade of irregular war when they had raided Kansas's abolitionist households and institutions, and in turn were attacked by their counterparts, such as John Brown and his sons; when the Civil War broke out, the opposing forces were Kansas anti-slavery guerrillas, called "Jayhawkers." Not only young men were combatants, but whole extended families and communities were involved, young women often as couriers, such as teenage Belle Starr.[8]

Missouri became a state of the United States in 1821, entering as a slave state, but it never formally seceded or joined the Confederate States of America. Both the Union and Confederacy claimed Missouri, which had two competing state governments and representatives in the U.S. Congress as well as in the Confederacy Congress. What became the state of Missouri had been a section of the French

Louisiana Territory that the Jefferson administration purchased from Napoleon in 1803. As with the founding of all the colonies before U.S. Independence, and of territories that would become states after Independence, settlers and their voluntary militias preceded the armies and administrators in displacing the Native population. In the case of Missouri, Daniel Boone, with his extended family and community, led Anglo-American settlement there, migrating from Kentucky when Missouri was still a part of the Spanish Empire; he had initiated settlement on Native land in Kentucky illegally under British law in 1769. Boone's group settled a swath along both sides of the part of the Missouri River, from St. Louis, on the confluence of the Missouri and Mississippi rivers, to Kansas City, at the western end of the Missouri River before it turns north, and this is where the Missouri Confederate guerrillas were born. Some of the area reached to the Missouri part of the Ozarks.[9]

In Missouri, there were no super-wealthy slave-worked cotton plantations with absentee owners, as there were in the Deep South, but the labor of enslaved Africans was often used in Missouri to commercially produce hemp, corn, wheat, oats, and rye. At the onset of the Civil War, enslaved Africans made up nearly 10 percent of the population in Missouri, while slavers were only 3 percent of the settler population. There were tensions between those who did and those who did not own property. Yet, if few Missouri families enslaved people compared to the numbers in the South, slavers were brutal and Black people were brutalized equally, if not more, after being freed.[10]

The August 1863 massacre in Lawrence, Kansas, led

by William Quantrill was one of many brutal attacks and counterattacks occurring at the time between those loyal to either abolitionism or slavery. Lawrence had become famous for being a militant anti-slavery bastion, founded by settlers from the Massachusetts Emigrant Aid Society soon after Kansas Territory was opened by the federal government in 1854. Pro-slavery Kansas settlers sacked and burned Lawrence in 1856, which set off months of guerrilla warfare, best remembered for the role of abolitionist John Brown and his sons.

William Quantrill was born in Ohio, made his living as a cattle rustler and slave catcher in Missouri-Kansas and Texas, and was living in Lawrence in 1859, although not yet politicized. Quantrill's pro-slavery terrorism in Missouri coincided with the onset of the Civil War, when he and fifteen men set out to torture, kill, and destroy the properties and livestock of abolitionists and their supporters. In August 1862, Quantrill received a field commission as a captain in the Confederate Army.[11]

By the time of the attack on Lawrence a year later, Quantrill was able to muster a force of hundreds of Bushwhacker guerrillas, nearly all armed with multiple six-shot revolvers. The group staged its attack at daybreak, when everyone in the town was still sleeping. Although the men of Lawrence had drilled and practiced for defending themselves and the town, they stored their firearms and ammunition in the city's armory, so the sleeping population was defenseless when the lightning attack began. Over a span of hours, the guerrillas secured the main hotel as a command center, slaughtering 150 unarmed men and boys, most of the adult males of the town. They burned about a quarter of the town's buildings, including all the businesses except two.[12]

For the city of Lawrence today, the trauma of the massacre still resonates, especially for the descendants of the dead and survivors. "'It was utterly catastrophic,' said Pat Kehde, a retired Lawrence bookstore owner and great-granddaughter of Ralph and Jetta Dix," reads a *Wichita Journal* account 150 years after the fact. "On the morning of the raid, Jetta tried to protect Ralph by standing between William Quantrill's men and her husband. When Jetta stumbled as one of Quantrill's men rode his horse into her, Ralph was momentarily unguarded and in that instant was shot and killed."[13] "We are in an age where we have a war on terrorism, and we talk about terrorism all the time," said Lawrence historian Paul Stuewe, "but we don't think about the 19th-century terrorism."[14] "It is a calamity of the most heartrending kind," said the *New York Times* following the attacks, "an atrocity of unspeakable character."[15]

Following the Civil War, John Newman Edwards, who had fought for the Confederacy, wrote *Noted Guerrillas*, extolling the Missouri guerrillas as great patriots of the Confederate cause, romanticizing the taking of life up close, claiming the guerrillas were almost superhuman specimens, trying to place them alongside the valiant Confederate Army to be commemorated. He was fascinated by the guerrillas' deft use of the pistol, often attacking with one in each hand, rather than a rifle, which was the standard weapon used by professional soldiers. He wrote that before a battle, "a Guerrilla takes every portion of his revolver apart and lays it upon a white shirt, if he has one, as carefully as a surgeon places his instruments on a white towel. . . . He touches each piece as a man might touch the thing that he loves."[16]

Edwards also portrayed Quantrill and his guerrillas as expert horsemen, shooting while riding fast. In fetishizing the guerrilla revolver and the horse, Edwards heralded the beginning of the "cowboy" and "outlaw" hero of the post–Civil War decades, even though these figures had nothing to do with cattle or ranching or even the "West."[17] Some of the most enduringly famous, or infamous, of the Missouri guerrillas—Jesse James, Cole Younger, Myra Maybelle Shirley (Belle Starr), and their brothers—came from land-owning slavers; some, like the Shirleys, ran successful business operations and were well connected politically. Their elevation to post–Civil War social bandit heroes would eclipse their former pro-Confederate deeds.[18] In the two decades after the Civil War, the Winchester rifle was fetishized for killing Indians, and the Colt revolver for outlawry. In the process, gun violence and civilian massacres were not just normalized, but commercially glorified, packaged, promoted, and mass marketed.

"In the annals of American frontier mythology, no two figures have become more synonymous with generic notions of the 'Wild West' than Billy the Kid and Jesse James,"[19] writes historian Matthew Christopher Hulbert, noting that people often confuse the two, especially by placing Jesse in New Mexico and other parts of the former Mexican territory. Their biographies were collapsed in the cheap Western novels that were popular the way movies and television were later. They were each assassinated within nine months of each other, July 1881 for Billy the Kid and April 1882 for

Jesse James. Billy was born Henry William McCarty to a single mom who was an Irish famine refugee in New York City. She took him to New Mexico, where she died. As an orphan kid, he worked as a cowboy on ranches, then as a gunman in the service of a rancher in the endemic Anglo ranch wars of the time. Billy was twenty-one when Sheriff Pat Garrett assassinated him. Jesse James was thirty-five when he was assassinated. They never crossed paths, as Billy was never outside New Mexico after he moved there, and Jesse never strayed far from the Missouri borderlands with Kansas and the Indian Territory (eastern Oklahoma) where he would hide out. Hulbert points out that through fiction and later film, Jesse James is merged, along with a handful of other Confederate guerrillas, into the "same abstracted geographical space (the 'West') during an equally abstracted period of time (when that ambiguous western locale was particularly 'Wild')." The most storied of the Missouri-guerrillas-turned-Western-outlaws besides Jesse James was his brother Frank—they made up the leadership of the "James Gang"—along with Cole Younger and his brothers—the "Younger Brothers," with whom the "Bandit Queen" Belle Starr rode.[20]

Of course, there were other gunslinging outlaws besides Billy the Kid who were not former Confederate guerrillas, such as Wild Bill Hickok, the Dalton Brothers, and many more. But, historian Hulbert is interested in understanding the cultural process by which Jesse James and, through his legend, the other Missouri guerrillas "came to exist symbolically, first in two places—Missouri and the Wild West—and then only in one: the West of the popular imagination."

Understanding this process is far more important than we might realize, for this is not merely a
process of westernization but, through it, "Amer-
icanization." Bloodthirsty Confederates are being
incorporated (and "made safe") via a process that
moves them west and buries them there—allowing
them to become larger-than-life legends of American machismo. With them gone, the Civil War can
safely remain the *civilized* test of American manhood, and the Wild West can become the *civilizing*
test of American manhood. In the end, then, both
"histories" become genres of American masculine
self-congratulation.[21]

In the mid-twentieth century, with real and fictional
Western heroics in decline, fetishization of guns and the
Second Amendment accelerated, along with mass shootings,
nearly all carried out by white men.

Jesse James lore contributes to the Americana so beloved in the culture, generating "gun culture," as does the
iconic figure of Daniel Boone, the commercial hunter who
trail-blazed across the Appalachian chain and into the Ohio
Country, illegally establishing a settlement in what would
become Kentucky, and then moved on to Missouri as one
of the first settlers before it became a state. Jesse's parents,
Robert and Zerelda James, moved from Kentucky in the
wake of Daniel Boone's trek there. Boone himself was of
Welsh heritage, born in Pennsylvania, but most of those
who followed his migration were Scots-Irish. Westward migration of Scots-Irish settlers represented a mass movement

between 1720 and the War of Independence; during the last two decades of the eighteenth century, first- and second-generation Ulster-Scots continued to migrate to the Ohio Valley, West Virginia, Kentucky, and Tennessee. Ulster-Scots cleared forests, built log cabins, killed Indians, and took their cultivated land; historian Carl Degler writes, "These hardy, God-fearing Calvinists made themselves into a veritable human shield of colonial civilization."[22]

Richard Slotkin finds the origin of U.S. nationalism in the late eighteenth-century treks of settlers over the Appalachian-Allegheny spine. Daniel Boone, he writes, "became the most significant, most emotionally compelling myth-hero of the early republic," the U.S. American hero as "the lover of the spirit of the wilderness, and his acts of love and sacred affirmation are acts of violence against that spirit and her avatars." In the twentieth century reformation of the archetype, promoted notably in the writings of Theodore Roosevelt and, of course, Western novels and films, Slotkin finds the "hunter" and the "farmer," or "breeder," and especially "the man who knows Indians."[23] Indeed, it is rare even today to meet a descendant of the old settler trekking culture who does not identify Daniel Boone as a direct ancestor.

Jesse James was sixteen years old in 1863 when he joined the Missouri pro-Confederate guerrillas; his older brother Frank was already an experienced member. Jesse had less than twenty years to live, in which time he became one of the most famous men alive. Among his mentors in his two years as a guerrilla was Archie Clements; together the two were involved in particularly gruesome killings, including mutilations of corpses. After the war ended, Clements led a group of former guerrillas, including Jesse, in an armed robbery of a bank. Soon Clements himself was murdered, and leadership fell to the now twenty-one-year-old Jesse James. By 1868, this group became known as the James-Younger Gang, with Jesse at its head, and included his brother Frank, Cole and Jim Younger, and four other former Confederate guerrillas. Two other Younger brothers, John and Bob, too young to be guerrillas during the war, also rode with the gang. They robbed banks and trains in Missouri, Kansas, Iowa, and Kentucky until 1876, when the enterprise crashed in a failed attempt to stick up a bank in Northfield, Minnesota. Several members of the gang were captured and sent to prison, including Cole and Jim Younger, but Jesse escaped. He tried, but failed, to form another gang, and lived the final six years of his life in the open in St. Joseph, Missouri, using the fake identity of a Mr. Howard, a horse trader. His assassin, Robert Ford, hired by the governor of Missouri, found and befriended him, then shot him dead in 1882.[24] In 2007, Hollywood revived Jesse as a lone hero in a critically acclaimed film, *The Assassination of Jesse James by the Coward Robert Ford*, starring Brad Pitt as Jesse and Casey Affleck as Ford.

In his biography of Jesse James, T.J. Stiles makes an important point about the guerrillas-to-outlaws period, observing that they emerged during a time of new mass-produced guns made with innovative technology, which were much more lethal but also more affordable than guns had ever been.

Before the Civil War, most firearms were hand-made by local gunsmiths. Rapid-firing handguns, designed to kill people, were relatively uncommon. There was so little demand for Samuel Colt's revolutionary revolver that his Patent Arms Manufacturing Company went bankrupt in 1843. The Civil War changed all that by putting firearms in the hands of millions of men, fostering mass production of revolvers, and launching a new marketing offensive by weapons makers. On May 5, 1865, with scattered skirmishes still flaring in Missouri, Secretary of War Edwin M. Stanton wired a striking message to the military commander there. 'Gun manufacturers are applying for leave to sell guns and ammunition to the loyal people of Missouri. . . . Is there any objections to opening the trade to the sale of fire-arms and ammunition, and under what restrictions if any?' There were neither objections nor limitations.[25]

During the Civil War's irregular warfare against non-combatants, citizens began to carry firearms, and gun violence and murder became commonplace. The normalization of violence included the racial terrorism of the KKK and other armed groups, as well as the outlaw violence carried out by individuals and crime gangs. Not surprisingly, many of the gunfights of the late nineteenth century in the West took place between Union and Confederate veterans or supporters. Ghosts of those battle lines can be detected in contemporary divisions on gun rights and gun control.[26] Today, one can see the Confederate battle flag unfurled at protests and rallies and at gun shows in South Carolina and Virginia, as well as in the Pacific Northwest or Chicago.

Former Confederate guerrillas jumped on the opportunity to join Theodore Roosevelt's "Rough Riders" in Cuba. Due to increasing insurrections of enslaved populations, in 1886 the Spanish Empire abolished legal slavery in Cuba. Spain had remained active in the transatlantic slave trade up to that time, and had transported a million enslaved Africans to Cuba. But by 1895, Afro-Cubans, along with Spanish-Cuban revolutionaries, had raised a full war of independence against Spain. They were on the cusp of victory in 1898, when they were crushed by the U.S. invasion and occupation. The United States falsely took credit for ousting Spain and "freeing" the Cuban people in what U.S. historians call the "Spanish-American War," next turning to the Philippines to neutralize their revolution against Spanish control.

When President William McKinley called for volunteers to fight in Cuba, future U.S. president Theodore Roosevelt, then assistant secretary of the Navy, resigned and dipped into his personal fortune to finance and outfit the First United States Volunteer Cavalry, one of three voluntary regiments raised for the invasion. The core troops that he outfitted were drawn from the Ninth Cavalry ("Buffalo Soldiers"), the segregated African American army regiment, but his call for volunteers was answered by many former Confederate and Union regular soldiers as well as guerrillas. Roosevelt borrowed the term "Rough Riders" from "Buffalo Bill's Wild West and Congress of Rough Riders of the World," melding war and show business. Out of the many thousands of men who volunteered, the thousand-plus whom Roosevelt chose came from Arizona, New Mexico, Oklahoma Territory, and Texas. The requirements included being good with guns and horses, and physically capable; most were working cowhands, prospectors, gamblers, hunters, lawmen, Civil War veterans, and former Confederate guerrillas.

In the fight, the presence of former Confederate and former Union soldiers and guerrillas, white and Black, even some Native Americans, all fighting on the same side under the U.S. flag, signaled a certain reconciliation: "To former Union vets, ex-Rebels carrying the American flag reiterated their victory in the Civil War. To former Confederates, the Spanish-American War was an invaluable opportunity to renew their status as citizens of the United States once and for all."[27] The Army became the institution that brought North and South together in militarism, and also the one that brought them to the cutting edge of racial and gender integration.

And so began the long twentieth century of endless U.S. wars, covert and open, with a distinct revival of gun glorification and a recasting of the personalities of brutal pro-slavery guerrillas as outlaw heroes, the influence of which continues to spill over into the present.

FIVE

MYTH OF THE HUNTER

Seventy-four percent of gun owners in the United States are male, and 82 percent of gun owners are white which means that 61 percent of all adults who own guns are white men, and this group accounts for 31 percent of the total U.S. population. The top reason U.S. Americans give for owning a gun is for protection.[1] What are the majority of white men so afraid of? Does anyone believe that centuries of racial and economic domination of the United States by white men have left no traces in our culture, views, or institutions? It's not likely, given all the evidence to the contrary. The ongoing influence of this history is compounded by the lack of acknowledgment of the colonists' savage violence across the continent that continued until the twentieth century, and the legacies of African slavery through such practices as convict leasing, legal segregation, rampant institutional racism, discrimination, police killings, mass surveillance, criminalization, and incarceration.

There is another historical paradigm that contributes to the white U.S. male's affinity for firearms, namely, "The

Hunter." Norman Mailer characterized this type in his 1948 war novel, *The Naked and the Dead*:

SAM CROFT

THE HUNTER

A lean man of medium height but he held himself so erectly he appeared tall. His narrow triangular face was utterly without expression. There seemed nothing wasted in his hard small jaw, gaunt firm cheeks and straight short nose. His gelid eyes were very blue. . . . He hated weakness and he loved practically nothing. There was a crude uniformed vision in his soul but he was rarely conscious of it. . . .

His ancestors pushed and labored and strained, drove their oxen, sweated their women, and moved a thousand miles.

He pushed and labored inside himself and smoldered with an endless hatred.[2]

Many people in the United States who have not grown up with guns appear to think that the Second Amendment and gun rights are about hunting; they are mystified as to why a semiautomatic AR-15 or an assault rifle might be needed for hunting. But gun affinity isn't about hunting, although it is related to the myth of the hunter.

Whereas white supremacy had been the working rationalization for British theft of Indigenous lands and for European enslavement of Africans, the bid for independence by what became the United States of America was more problematic. Democracy, equality, and equal rights do not fit well with genocide, settler colonialism, slavery, and empire. It was during the 1820s—the beginning of Andrew Jackson's era of populist settler-democracy, called "The Age of Democracy" by many U.S. historians—that the unique U.S. origin narratives evolved reconciling rhetoric with reality. Novelist James Fenimore Cooper was among its initial scribes.

Cooper's reinvention of the birth of the United States in his novel *The Last of the Mohicans* became and has remained the populist U.S. origin story. Herman Melville called Cooper "our national novelist."[3] Cooper was the wealthy son of a U.S. congressman, a land speculator who built Cooperstown, named after himself, in upstate New York, where James grew up, on land taken from the Haudenosaunee. His hometown was christened all-American with the establishment of the National Baseball Hall of Fame there during the Depression year of 1936. Expelled from Yale, Cooper did a stint in the U.S. Navy, then married and began writing. From 1823 to 1841, he published the five books in his Leatherstocking Tales series, beginning with *The Pioneers*, followed by *The Last of the Mohicans*, *The Prairie*, *The Pathfinder*, and *The Deerslayer*. Each featured the character Natty Bumppo, also called variously, depending on his age, Leatherstocking, Pathfinder, or Deerslayer. Bumppo is a British settler on land appropriated from the Delaware Nation and is buddies with its fictional Delaware leader Chingachgook (the "last Mohican" in the myth). Together the Leatherstocking Tales narrate the mythical forging of the new country from the

1754–63 French and Indian War in *The Last of the Mohicans* to the settlement of the plains by migrants traveling by wagon train from Kentucky and Tennessee. At the end of the saga, Bumppo dies a very old man on the edge of the Rocky Mountains, as he gazes east.

The Last of the Mohicans, published in 1826, was a best seller throughout the nineteenth century and has been in print continuously since. Two Hollywood movies were based on the story, the most recent made in 1992, the Columbus Quincentennial. Cooper devised a fictional counterpoint of celebration to the dark underbelly of the new American nation—the birth of something new and wondrous, literally, the U.S. American race, a new people born of the merger of the best of both worlds, the Native and the European, not a biological merger but something more ephemeral, involving the disappearance of the Indian. In the novel, Cooper has the last of the "noble" and "pure" Natives die off, with the "last Mohican" handing the continent over to Hawkeye, the nativized settler, his adopted son. This convenient fantasy could be seen as quaint at best, were it not for its deadly staying power. Cooper had much to do with creating the U.S. origin myth that generations of historians and textbooks have dedicated themselves to rationalizing. In the process, he fortified the U.S. American exceptionalism that weaves through much of the literature produced in the United States (not only the writing of historians) and is parroted by anyone who wishes to excel in politics, the military, or academia—and even by poets, from Walt Whitman to the Beats of the 1950s. The late writer Wallace Stegner decried the devastation wrought by U.S. domination and destruction of Indigenous peoples, wildlife, and the land, but reinforced the idea of U.S. exceptionalism by reducing colonization to a twist of fate that produced some charming if confounding characteristics:

> Ever since Daniel Boone took his first excursion over Cumberland Gap, Americans have been wanderers. . . . With a continent to take over and Manifest Destiny to goad us, we could not have avoided being footloose. The initial act of emigration from Europe, an act of extreme, deliberate disaffiliation, was the beginning of a national habit.
>
> It should not be denied, either, that being footloose has always exhilarated us. It is associated in our minds with escape from history and oppression and law and irksome obligations, with absolute freedom, and the road has always led west. Our folk heroes and our archetypal literary figures accurately reflect that side of us. Leatherstocking, Huckleberry Finn, the narrator of Moby Dick, all are orphans and wanderers; any of them could say, "Call me Ishmael." The Lone Ranger has no dwelling place except the saddle.[4]

The publication of Cooper's *Leatherstocking Tales* paralleled the presidency of Andrew Jackson. For those who consumed the books in that period and throughout the nineteenth century, the novels became perceived fact, not fiction, and the basis for the coalescence of U.S. civil religion and nationalism—Americanism, white nationalism.

Behind the legend was a looming real-life figure, the archetype that inspired the stories, namely, Daniel Boone, an icon of U.S. settler colonialism. Boone's life spanned nearly a century, 1734 to 1820, precisely the period covered in the Leatherstocking series. Boone was born in Berks County, Pennsylvania, on the edge of British settlement. He is an avatar of the moving colonial-Indigenous frontier. To the west lay "Indian Country," claimed through the Doctrine of Discovery by both Britain and France but free of Europeans save for a few traders, trappers, and soldiers manning colonial outposts.

Daniel Boone died in 1820 in Missouri, a part of the vast territory acquired in the 1803 Louisiana Purchase. When the Spanish opened Missouri in 1799 for foreigners to settle, the Boone family led the way. Yet, decades later, his body was taken for burial to Frankfort, Kentucky, the cultish covenant heart of the Ohio Country—Indian Country—for which the Revolution had been fought and in which he had been the trekker superhero, almost a deity.

Daniel Boone was re-created as a celebrity at age fifty in 1784, a year after the end of the War of Independence. Real estate speculator John Filson, seeking settlers to buy unceded land in the Ohio Country, although it was still densely populated with Native towns and farms, wrote and self-published *The Discovery, Settlement and Present State of Kentucke*, along with a map to guide the intruders. The book contained an appendix about Daniel Boone, purportedly written by Boone himself, but surely written by Filson, as Boone is not known to have ever written anything, although he was literate. That part of the book on Boone's "adventures" subsequently was published as "The Adventures of Col. Daniel Boone" in the *American Magazine* in 1787, then as a book. Thereby a star was born—the mythical hero, the hunter, the "Man Who Knows Indians," as Richard Slotkin has described this U.S. American archetype:

> The myth of the hunter that had grown up about the figure of Filson's Daniel Boone provided a framework within which Americans attempted to define their cultural identity, social and political values, historical experience, and literary aspirations. . . . Daniel Boone, Washington, Franklin, and Jefferson were heroes to the whole nation because their experiences had reference to many or all of these common experiences. "The Hunters of Kentucky," a popular song that swept the nation in 1822–28, helped elect Andrew Jackson as President by associating him with Boone, the hero of the West.[5]

Yet the Leatherstocking's positive twist on genocidal colonialism was based on the reality of invasion squatting, attacking, and colonizing the land and people of Indigenous nations. Neither Filson nor Cooper created that reality. Rather, they created the mythological narratives that captured the experience and imagination of the Anglo-American settler, stories that were surely instrumental in sanitizing accountability for the atrocities related to genocide, and set the narrative pattern for future U.S. writers, poets, and historians.

What Daniel Boone, like George Washington, was up

to was intruding upon sovereign Native land so as to covertly survey it and sell it to white settlers, who would then form themselves into militias to murder the families who had been living there for generations. Some were successful and grew rich and powerful, such as George Washington, while others, like Boone, never attained wealth, his land speculations resulting in bankruptcy. Regarding Boone's hunting career, it was purely commercial; he killed animals not for food, but to sell their pelts for profit. Boone made a modest living as a market hunter. Annually, trekking alone or in small groups of other market hunters, he would go on "long hunts"—months-long expeditions into unceded Indian hunting grounds. Collecting hundreds of buck deer skins in the autumn, he would then trap beaver and otter for their valuable pelts over the winter. In the Spring, market hunters returned to sell their bounty to commercial fur traders. In this business, buckskins came to be known as "bucks," originating the slang term for "dollar."[6] But the legend and lore that mushroomed around Daniel Boone advanced notions of the hero explorer and adventurous hunter, and were written over the fact that he was a merchant, a trader, a land speculator, and a failed businessman.

Theodore Roosevelt wrote, "No form of labor is harder than the chase, nor none so excellent as a training school for war. . . . A race of peaceful, unwarlike farmers would have been helpless before such foes as the red Indians. . . . Colonists fresh from the old world, no matter how thrifty, steady-going, and industrious, could not hold their own on the frontier; they had to settle where they were protected from the Indians by a living barrier of bold and self-reliant

American borderers." But Roosevelt warned of a class difference among these border militias, writing, "All qualities, good and bad, are intensified and accentuated in the life of the wilderness."[7] Of course, from his point of view, his kind—wealthy Anglo-Saxons—had all the good qualities.

Roosevelt was vice president of the United States when President William McKinley was assassinated in 1901; he became president at age forty-two, served out the rest of McKinley's term, and was re-elected. Roosevelt was already a national hero for having led the irregular volunteers to fight the Spanish in Cuba alongside regular U.S. Army soldiers and Marines. During the previous adult years of his life, Roosevelt forged a renewed myth of "The Hunter."

Roosevelt was born in 1858 in New York City, son of a wealthy businessman and a wealthy socialite mother from Georgia, his father descended from the original Dutch settlers in New York. They were related to an upstate New York slave-trading family, the Schuylers, the family Alexander Hamilton married into, then came to manage the family's slave trade.[8] Roosevelt was a sickly asthmatic child who early on turned to strenuous physical activity to overcome his weakness. He seemed headed for a life in academia or law, tutored at home, then graduating from Harvard, then Columbia Law School, marrying into the wealthy Cabot Lodge family (whose wealth came from the Atlantic slave trade), researching and writing books, as well as traveling extensively. But early on, he was attracted to politics and later claimed that it was while in law school that he decided he wanted "to be one of the governing class."[9]

Roosevelt's first interest was naval power, about which

he researched and published, gaining recognition as a naval historian. However, he became obsessed with the Anglo-Saxon conquest of what became the United States, and during the decade 1885 to 1894, published the seven-volume *The Winning of the West*. During that time, he purchased and operated a cattle ranch in North Dakota where he spent a good deal of time learning to be a rancher and trophy hunter; he wrote and published three books on hunting, proud that he had helped in the slaughter of the bison, the life sustenance of the Plains peoples. He even became a deputy sheriff and chased outlaws. He began to consider himself an heir to the hunter icons such as Daniel Boone and Davy Crockett, another mythologized figure, who died at the Alamo.

In 1887, Roosevelt and his closest family friend and political ally, Henry Cabot Lodge, founded the Boone and Crockett Club for trophy hunters like themselves. The membership included politicians, professionals, and businessmen, as well the famous painters of the romanticized West, Albert Bierstadt and Frederic Remington, and the popular Western novelist Owen Wister.[10] Roosevelt was an early convert to "Social Darwinism," leading to the racist pseudo-science of eugenics. In his view, all the darker peoples were inferior, particularly Native Americans, who were destined to disappear completely. But he also regarded poor whites as inferior, and distinguished himself from those "game butchers" who hunt and kill animals for profit or to eat. He identified with Cooper's character Hawkeye and embraced the Boone myth, as men killed only to test and prove their manhood. Roosevelt's hunting was for aristocrats, to revitalize the superior class of the species. Furthermore, he theorized that a new race was born with testing of settlers' survival skills in nature, creating a new kind of aristocracy destined to rule the world. The settler "stock" that morphed into that superior species was composed of English, Scots-Irish, French Huguenots, German, and Dutch, all Protestants.[11]

However lowly and savage on Roosevelt's scale, Native communities played a key role in his theory of the genesis of white supremacy. Roosevelt argued that the superior European was strengthened by not intermarrying with their defeated enemies, which would cause loss of vigor. Slotkin summarizes the genocidal violence inherent in the perspective: "American settlers must regain that vigor by repelling and exterminating their barbarians. Instead of biological exchange with savages of another race or folk, the Americans participate in a *spiritual* exchange, taking from the enemy certain abstract ideas or principle but accepting no admixture of blood." The settlers must become "men who know Indians," embracing the "savage" rules of warfare that it takes to destroy the enemy. But Roosevelt also drew inspiration from Native territorial sovereignty, particularly the Haudenosaunee and their insistence on maintaining their lands, providing a model for U.S. American nationalism.

Richard Slotkin views overseas U.S. imperialism, of which Theodore Roosevelt was a major booster and actor, as a "regeneration through violence," or recovering the frontier spirit, becoming the hunter, the martial tradition that goes to the root of the founding of the United States and continues today. The process of extension, both as doctrine and as violence, is ongoing, and does much to explain the continuing affinity for guns among those who identify with the masculinized and racialized white nationalist narratives of Americana, revering the Second Amendment as its crown jewel.

In a 2016 *New York Times* opinion piece on free trade agreements and deindustrialization in coal country, rural Kentucky writer and self-identified "Second Amendment person" Daniel Hayes makes a compelling point about the symbolism of possessing firearms: "In the heartland, these are people who feel they've been the victims of sustained economic violence at the hands of tyrannical governments of both parties. In 2008, Barack Obama's notorious misstep got one thing right: Rural people will 'cling' to guns. Not because they are sad or misguided, but because it is the last right they feel they still have: a liberty at least, in place of opportunity."[12] After narrating the painful dysfunctional economic and social conditions in rural Kentucky, along with the de-peopling of the region, particularly the flight of youth, he continues, "Outsourcing and guns: These are the twin issues animating Trump voters in rural Kentucky. The two are linked and feed off each other; the only difference between them is that white rural voters see outsourcing as a losing battle, whereas protecting and expanding Second Amendment rights is the only policy they've been able to get politicians to move on. For that reason alone, it is totemic."[13]

There's a sense of victimization in the essay that's prevalent among the descendants of the early Anglo settlers who were on the losing side of capitalist rapaciousness. When Robert Schenkkan's *The Kentucky Cycle*,[14] won the Pulitzer Prize in 1992, Kentucky intellectuals and writers took notice and were outraged. *The Kentucky Cycle* is a collection of nine interconnected plays that requires nearly seven hours of stage time for its production and had premiered in Seattle, becoming the first Pulitzer drama award to go to a play that had not first opened in New York. The narrative follows one settler family and its descendants in eastern Kentucky's Appalachia over a period of two hundred years, from first settlement in 1775 to 1975, during the waning days of being the center of the coal mining industry and the beginning of massive deindustrialization in the United States. Schenkkan stresses that the "land" itself is a major character.[15] It is in this manner that he reflects on the violent expulsion of the Indigenous Cherokee farmers; the degradation of the land by commercial, albeit small-scale, slave-worked, monocrop agriculture; commercial cutting of the trees and killing (mostly by trapping) wildlife that caused erosion, destitution, and the exhaustion of the land; the inability of small operators to compete with the large slave-worked plantations and were forced to migrate to Missouri; and, after the Civil War, the introduction of underground coal mining, the demise of the industry, and massive unemployment. Schenkkan concludes the play with the War on Poverty and the Vista volunteer program for the jobless and hungry residents.

Bobbie Ann Mason, a celebrated fiction writer, essayist, and literary critic from Kentucky, interviewed Schenkkan and wrote a sharply critical essay in *The New Yorker* in 1993. Mason's first novel, *In Country*, dealing with Vietnam veterans who come home to Appalachia, was made into a major Hollywood film in 1989. Schenkkan told Mason that the core value he saw in his play was larger than Kentucky: "One of our big problems is how much we're in denial about our past, and how unwilling we are to examine our past and to come to terms with it. There's so much loss in this country, so much grief that we're in denial about. There's a river of loss that runs through the bedrock of this country. . . . What I am interested in is how much Eastern Kentucky's situation, which can be viewed, and has historically been viewed, as somewhat isolated, is in fact really a paradigm for the United States as a whole."[16]

This is exactly what University of Kentucky professor and writer Gurney Norman hated most about Schenkkan's play. Norman, who grew up in the eastern Kentucky Appalachian coal country, was one of its most vocal critics. "I know the story of Appalachia deep in my bones," writes Norman, "I have immersed myself in it all my adult life, and to see Robert Schenkkan run roughshod over a whole culture is very upsetting."[17] He was most upset by Schenkkan's use of Kentucky as a stand-in for the United States as a whole, saying, "The play imposes the form of classical tragedy—where people bring about their own downfall— on the history of the region. . . . It blames the victim," while reducing the people and the place to embodiments of violence and greed. But Professor Norman goes on to express a larger theme, one of "political correctness," an accusation that was just taking off in the early 1990s: "'The Kentucky Cycle' is a very politically correct play. . . . It's revisionist history. . . . The old American dream of the frontier is replaced by a vision of butchers and murderers. . . . The vicious hatred of America is very prevalent today."[18] So Professor Norman actually appears to see Kentucky as representative of the nation.

Mason ends her long essay by seemingly referring to the "lost cause" of the Civil War that continues to divide North and South: "In the country, when two farmers can't agree to maintain a common fence, each man builds a fence on his own land. They have a name for the space left between the two fences. They call it the Devil's lane."[19]

This denial of the past is not unique to Kentucky or Appalachia, but rather reflective of U.S. settler-colonialism moving from the original thirteen colonies following the War of Independence. Kentucky was the navel of that process and Daniel Boone its mythologized figure—Daniel Boone, "the hunter."

Another of Daniel Hayes's essays, "Why I Hunt," reflects an even deeper symbolism and mythology of guns that is a part of the Kentucky story and part of the national story. Hayes tells of the first shot he ever fired while hunting, his distance from the prey—a white-tail buck—being the length of a football field and a half, viewed through his rifle's scope. On a snowy January day, he writes, "One grand buck and his ladies and children moved nervously on a white background. They bunched together, the big male turned his head this way and that . . . moving as one. . . . I pulled the trigger and the buck rolled back to his left. He took a half dozen staggered bounding steps, fell, and lay still in the snow. As the adrenaline died down I started coming to myself again."[20] Hayes tells of butchering the deer, putting aside the hide for tanning: "I recall a feeling of deep symbiosis. . . . I felt 'not alone.' . . . It felt like a ritual and I felt like I was not alone. . . . It made real for me the truth that for every thing that lives on this planet something else must die and it made real the truth that this animal's life was saving me from death. I hunt and I'll keep hunting."

Hayes gives even more specific reasons why he hunts: "I hunt because I'm an environmentalist and conservationist. I hunt because I believe that I'm closer to the Earth when engaging with it and there's something at stake. . . . Something could very well die. In fact, that's the goal." But he abhors industrial meat production: "What I do is the antithesis of the stockyard. It's the key to that imprisoning gate. . . . I hunt for love and I hunt to escape. . . . I hunt for competence, discipline, and craft."[21]

These words echo from the narratives created by the real estate entrepreneur John Filson about Daniel Boone in Kentucky. But Boone was an industrial hunter. Like him, most of the settlers who hunted and the famed "mountain men" of the West, they set traps to capture animals for their fur. They killed for pelts, not for food, not for love of nature. The central role that the myth of the hunter continues to play in Americana is to perpetuate the contemporary romance with firearms and justification for the sacredness of the Second Amendment, eclipsing the fact that this was a capitalist enterprise carried out through atrocities of violence, territorial theft, and mass displacement, not an adventure.

SIX

THE SECOND AMENDMENT AS A COVENANT

The Mayflower Compact, the Declaration of Independence, the United States Constitution, the writings of the "Founding Fathers," Lincoln's Gettysburg Address, the "Star-Spangled Banner," the Pledge of Allegiance, the flag,[1] Columbus Day, Thanksgiving, Fourth of July, the Second Amendment, and even Martin Luther King Jr.'s "I Have a Dream" speech are all bundled as sacred fetishes[2] and rituals that comprise the U.S. state doctrine—American Exceptionalism—which is capable of absorbing and adjusting to disruptive cultural and political changes, such as by taming Dr. King's radicalism. An aspect of this most visible today is the all-powerful "gun lobby," whose members are devoted to the presumed sanctity of the Second Amendment. In the forefront of these Second Amendment adherents are the descendants of the old British and Northern European settlers who say that they represent "The People" and have the right to bear arms, the right to have military bases around the world, and the right—even the duty—to overthrow any government that does not, in their view, adhere to the God-given covenant.[3]

In a satirical essay written following the Orlando night-club mass killing that took forty-nine lives, historian and theologian Garry Wills concluded that gun control in the United States is "inconceivable."

> And it is historically inconceivable—everyone knows that guns are what made this country great, taming the West, keeping up our fighting spirit, shoving sissies aside as we make our tough progress.

> It is also theologically inconceivable. God gave us guns to show us who we are. Giving up the gun would be surrender to evil, taking us abruptly into eschatological time.

> So this time let us skip all the sighing and promising and moments of silence. Why keep up the pretense that we are going to take any real and practical steps toward sanity? Everyone knows we are not going to do a single damn thing. We can't. We are captives of The Gun.

> The Gun is patriotic.

> The Gun is America.

> The Gun is God.[4]

According to the founding narratives of the United States, colonists from Europe acquired a vast expanse of land from a scattering of benighted peoples who lacked a concept of private property, and therefore could claim no right, in any Western sense, to the land. The historical record is clear, however, that English colonizers aggressively displaced a large network of small and large nations whose governments, commerce, arts and sciences, agriculture, technologies, theologies, philosophies, and institutions were intricately developed. These nations maintained sophisticated relations with one another and with the environments that supported them; they were stewards of one of the seven locales of agricultural civilization, which they created over tens of thousands of years. Many have noted that had North America been an unpopulated wilderness, undeveloped, without roads, and uncultivated, it might still be so, for the European colonists could not have survived without forcibly appropriating the Indigenous peoples' developed lands and resources. They appropriated what had already been created by Indigenous civilizations. They stole already cultivated farmland and the corn, vegetables, tobacco, cotton, and other crops domesticated centuries before the arrival of European invaders who took control of the deer parks that had been cleared and maintained by Indigenous communities, used existing roads and water routes in order to move armies to conquer, and relied on captured Indigenous people to identify the locations of water, oyster beds, and medicinal herbs.

The United States is not unique among nations in forging origin myths, but one of the few in which its citizens seem to believe it to be exceptional by grace of the Creator, and this exceptionalist ideology has been used to justify genocide, appropriation of the continent, and then domination of the rest of the world. Other such exceptionalist national entities are Israel and the now defunct apartheid state of South Africa, both of which were founded in 1948, as well as the Ulster-Scots colony of Northern Ireland. None of these, however, openly pursued global "full-spectrum dominance" by formal military doctrine, as has the United States.[5] The origin narratives of these colonizers are based on Judeo-Christian scripture, but the states they founded were not theocracies. According to their narratives, the faithful citizens come together of their own free will and pledge to each other and to their god to form and support a godly society, and their god, in turn, vouchsafes them prosperity in a promised land.

The influence of scriptures was pervasive among many of the Western social and political thinkers whose ideas the founders of the first British colonies in North America drew upon. Historian Donald Harman Akenson points to the way that "certain societies, in certain eras of their development," have looked to the scriptures for guidance, and likens it to the way "the human genetic code operates physiologically. That is, this great code has, in some degree, directly determined what people would believe and what they would think and what they would do." Dan Jacobson, a citizen of Boer-ruled South Africa, whose parents were immigrants, observes that, "like the Israelites, and their fellow Calvinists in New England, [the Boers] believed that they had been called by their God to wander through the wilderness, to meet and defeat the heathen, and to occupy a promised land on his behalf."[6]

Founders of the first North American colonies and later of the United States had a similar sense of a providential opportunity to make history. Indeed, as Akenson reminds us, "it is from [the] scriptures that western society learned how to think historically." The key moment in history, according to covenant ideology, "involves the winning of 'the Land' from alien, and indeed evil, forces."[7]

The principal conduit of the Hebrew Scriptures and covenant ideology for Christians was John Calvin, the French religious reformer whose teachings coincided with the advent of the British invasion and colonization of Ireland. English Puritan settlers drew upon Calvinist ideology in founding the Massachusetts Bay colony, as did the Dutch Calvinist settlers of the Cape of Good Hope in founding their South African colony during the same period. In accord with the doctrine of predestination, Calvin taught that human free will did not exist. Certain individuals are "called" by God and are among the "elect." Salvation therefore has nothing to do with one's actions; one is born as part of the elect or not, according to God's will. Individuals could never know for certain if they were among the elect, but outward good fortune, especially material wealth, was taken to be a manifestation of "election"; conversely, bad fortune and poverty, not to speak of dark skin, were taken as evidence of damnation. "The attractiveness of such a doctrine to a group of invading colonists . . . is obvious," Akenson observes, "for one could easily define the natives as immutably profane, and damned, and oneself as predestined to virtue."[8]

The U.S. Constitution represents for many citizens a covenant with God, and the covenant concept goes back to the Mayflower Compact, the first governing document of the Plymouth Colony, named for the ship that carried the hundred or so passengers to what is now Cape Cod, Massachusetts, in November 1620. Forty-one of the "Pilgrims," all men, wrote and signed the compact. Invoking God's name and declaring themselves loyal subjects of the king, the signatories announced that they had journeyed there "to plant the First Colony" and did therefore "Covenant and Combine ourselves together in a Civil Body Politic" to be governed by "just and equal Laws" enacted "for the general good of the Colony, unto which we promise all due submission and obedience."

The original Puritan settlers of Massachusetts Bay Colony, founded in 1630, adopted an official seal designed in England before their journey. The central image depicts a near-naked native holding a harmless, flimsy-looking bow and arrow and inscribed with the plea, "Come over and help us."[9] Nearly three hundred years later, the official seal of the U.S. military veterans of the "Spanish-American War" (the invasion and occupation of Puerto Rico, Cuba, and the Philippines) showed a naked woman kneeling before an armed U.S. soldier and a sailor, with a U.S. battleship in the background. One may trace this recurrent altruistic theme into the early twenty-first century, when the United States still invades countries under the guise of rescue, calling it "humanitarian intervention."

British settlers in North America brought with them the covenant ideology of Calvinism that had been the work of the Scotsman John Knox. John Locke, also a Scot, would later secularize the covenant idea into a "contract"—the "social contract"—whereby individuals sacrifice their liberty only through consent. Adam Smith, another Scot, during the period of the founding of the United States further developed Locke's theories, which were embraced by the "founding fathers," so that the U.S. republic became the first independent nation state founded on the ideology of capitalism, of land as a commodity.[10]

In other modern constitutional states, constitutions come and go, and they are never considered sacred in the manner patriotic U.S. citizens venerate theirs. Great Britain has no written constitution. The Magna Carta is an important and inspiring historical document, but it does not reflect a covenant. U.S. citizens did not inherit their cult-like adherence to their constitution from the English. From the Pilgrims to the "founders" of the United States and continuing to the present, the cultural persistence of the covenant idea of exceptionalism, and thus the bedrock of U.S. patriotism, represents a deviation from the main course in the development of national identities. Both the 1948 birth of the state of Israel and the advent of Nationalist Party rule in South Africa were emulations of the U.S. founding; certainly many U.S. Americans, particularly evangelical Protestants, closely identify with the state of Israel, as they did with Afrikaner-ruled South Africa. Patriotic U.S. politicians and citizens take pride in exceptionalism. Historians and legal theorists characterize U.S. statecraft and empire as those of a "nation of laws," rather than one dominated by a particular class or group of interests, suggesting a kind of purity or quasi-holiness.

Parallel to the idea of the U.S. Constitution as covenant, politicians, journalists, teachers, and even professional historians chant like a mantra that the United States is a "nation of immigrants." From its beginning, the United States has welcomed—indeed, often solicited, and promising "free land," even bribed—immigrants to populate conquered territories "cleansed" of their Indigenous inhabitants. From the mid-nineteenth century, immigrants were recruited to work in mines, raze forests, construct canals and railroads, and labor in sweatshops, factories, and commercial farm fields. In the late twentieth century, technical and medical workers were recruited. The requirements for citizenship mandate adherence to the Constitution through taking the Citizenship Oath, which involves swearing to "bear arms on behalf of the United States when required by the law . . . so help me God." Yet no matter how much immigrants might strive to prove themselves to be faithful and patriotic, and despite the rhetoric of *E pluribus unum*, their historical role is different from that of the colonial settlers who founded the republic. The original settlers are those who fought in the fifteen-year war for independence from Britain, but also, and perhaps more important, those who fought and shed Indian blood, before and after Independence, in order to gain possession of land; these were English Pilgrims, the Scots-Irish, and French Huguenots, Calvinists all, but also German Moravians and English Quakers, who took the land they believed had been bequeathed to them in the sacred covenant that predated the creation of the independent United States. These were the settlers who fought their way over the Appalachians into the fertile Ohio Valley region, and it is they who claimed blood sacrifice for their country. This remains the ideology that rules the United States.

New evangelical offshoots refashioned Calvinist

doctrines to do away with church hierarchies and decentralize. Frontier settlers continued to regard themselves as chosen people of the covenant, commanded by God to go into the wilderness to build the new Israel, and many towns in the United States, like Bethlehem, Pennsylvania, reflect this fervor with their Biblical names. Many settlers saw themselves, as their descendants see themselves, as the true and authentic patriots, specially endowed individuals entitled to the land through their blood sacrifice. The land won through bloodshed was not necessarily conceived in terms of particular parcels for a farm that would be passed down through generations. Most of the settlers who fought for it kept moving on nearly every generation. Land was property and interchangeable with other tracts of land for commercial agriculture. In the South many lost their holdings to land companies that then sold the land to slavers seeking to increase the size of their plantations. Without the unpaid labor of enslaved Africans, a farmer growing cash crops could not compete on the market. Once in the hands of settlers, the land itself was no longer sacred, as it had been for the Indigenous. Rather, it was private property, a commodity from which to earn profit—capable of making a man a king, or at least wealthy. Later, when Euro Americans had occupied the continent and urbanized much of it, this quest for land and the sanctity of private property were reduced to a lot with a house on it, and "the land" came to mean the country, the flag, the military, as in "the land of the free" of the national anthem, or Woody Guthrie's "This Land Is Your Land." Those who died fighting in foreign wars were said to have sacrificed their lives to protect "this land" that the old settlers had spilled blood to acquire. Expunged from national memory is that the majority of the blood spilled was that of Indigenous families.

These then were the settlers upon which the national origin narrative is based, the ultimately dispensable cannon fodder for the taking of the land and the continent, the white foot soldiers of empire, the "yeoman farmers" romanticized by Thomas Jefferson. They were not of the ruling class, but a few slipped through and later were drawn into it as elected officials and military officers, thereby maintaining the facade of a classless society and a democratic empire. The founders were English patricians, slavers, large agribusiness operators, or otherwise successful businessmen thriving on the slave trade, exports produced by enslaved Africans, and property sales. After Independence, when descendants of the common settlers—overwhelmingly Presbyterian or otherwise Calvinist Protestant—were accepted into the ruling class, they usually became Episcopalians, members of the elite church linked to the state Church of England.[11]

The Second Amendment is one of ten amendments comprising the original "bill of rights" for individual citizens that were added to the completed U.S. Constitution. The First Amendment, "freedom of speech," is most revered, and is considered an attribute of U.S. exceptionalism. The Second Amendment was drafted by James Madison and added to the U.S. Constitution in 1781. Little attention was paid to the Second Amendment until it became controversial during the second half of the twentieth century, and it continues coinciding with political, social, and economic shifts that opened nearly everything to question in the 1960s, particularly segregation and anti-Black racism. Then in the 1970s and 1980s, some white men, increasingly buttressed by the National Rifle Association, began pointing to the Second Amendment as an absolute right for the individual to bear arms and as justification for limiting firearms regulation, raising gun ownership as a constitutional issue, a covenant matter. On the National Rifle Association's website, every possible argument for gun control is contested based on the exact wording of the Second Amendment, in part by quoting the founders:

> George Mason asked, "[W]ho are the militia? They consist now of the whole people."

> Thomas Jefferson said, "No free man shall be debarred the use of arms."

> Patrick Henry said, "The great object is, that every man be armed."

> Richard Henry Lee wrote that, "to preserve liberty it is essential that the whole body of people always possess arms."

> Thomas Paine noted, "[A]rms . . . discourage and keep the invader and the plunderer in awe, and preserve order in the world as well as property."

> Samuel Adams warned, "The said Constitution [must] be never construed to authorize Congress to infringe the just liberty of the press, or the rights of conscience; or to prevent the people of the United

States, who are peaceable citizens, from keeping their own arms."[12]

Up to the 1970s, there had been little juridical attention paid to the Second Amendment, and it was not held to be sacrosanct by anyone, its mandate being taken for granted. In 1876, while the U.S. Army of the West was slaughtering Plains peoples and the buffalo with thousands of Winchesters, the Supreme Court ruled in *United States v. Cruikshank* that "the right to bear arms is not granted by the Constitution; neither is it in any manner dependent upon that instrument for its existence." There was no recorded negative reaction to that decision. A second Supreme Court decision in 1939, *United States v. Miller*, ruled that the federal government and the states could limit any weapon types not having a "reasonable relationship to the preservation or efficiency of a well regulated militia." Various regulations ensued in subsequent decades. But, following some forty years of political lobbying and challenging regulations, in 2008 the Supreme Court handed down a landmark decision, *District of Columbia v. Heller*, that held the Second Amendment protects an individual right to possess and carry firearms, the late Justice Antonin Scalia writing for the majority. For the first time, the highest court, the ultimate interpreter of the meaning of the United States Constitution, decided that the Second Amendment means "the individual" when it says "people." However, the decision left open the issue of government regulations: "[N]othing in our opinion should be taken to cast doubt on longstanding prohibitions on the possession of firearms by felons and the mentally ill, or laws forbidding the carrying of firearms in sensitive places such as schools and government buildings, or laws imposing conditions and qualifications on the commercial sale of arms."[13]

A Gallup poll released soon after the *Heller* decision found that 73 percent of those polled—a far larger percentage than gun owners or N.R.A. members—believed that the Second Amendment guarantees individual gun rights, while 20 percent believed it only guarantees the rights of state militia members. Only 7 percent had no opinion.[14] But, overwhelmingly, U.S. citizens, not only white men or the N.R.A., accept the notion of sanctity associated with the Second Amendment, as with the Constitution as a whole. The lobbying efforts of the N.R.A. and advertising by U.S. gun manufacturers are the designated culprits in most arguments for gun regulations and bans of some weapons, but the N.R.A. and gun manufacturers' success is due to a larger ideological hegemony that they did not create, but rather have exploited.

The majority argument in the *Heller* case is an example of the "originalism" that began as a marginal concept, slowly growing into a movement during the 1980s when conservative judges were appointed under the twelve-year stretch of the Ronald Reagan–George H.W. Bush administrations. The beginning of the movement is attributed to a speech in 1971 by the late Robert Bork, "Neutral Principles and Some First Amendment Problems."[15] Judge Bork was a professor of law at Yale and had served in government as Solicitor General and a judge of the U.S. Court of Appeals for the District of Columbia. President Ronald Reagan nominated him to the U.S. Supreme Court in 1987, but the Senate, with a Democratic majority, rejected the nomination. Civil Rights and women's groups lobbied against Bork's appointment, based on his record of having opposed federal intervention in enforcing voting rights in states and his call for annulling previous Supreme Court decisions on Civil Rights. However, Bork did not interpret the Second Amendment as applying to individuals and was critical of the National Rifle Association for promoting it as such.[16] Bork was far surpassed during the following two decades by even more extreme judges, particularly Scalia, relying on originalism and gutting the Voting Rights Act, abortion rights, and affirmative action. But by the end of the Reagan presidency the Conservative movement, buttressed by a large evangelical constituency, had reached critical mass; Supreme Court decisions and legislation followed.

The genealogy of the ascension of constitutional "originalism" begins with the 1954 Supreme Court decision to desegregate schools,[17] with opposing arguments in favor of "states' rights" and anti-communism. White Citizens Councils formed in the Southern states, along with other such groups, labeling all policies and acts of desegregation as communist-inspired. The John Birch Society, birthed in 1958 in Massachusetts by the scion of the Welch candy fortune, produced an ideology, a plan of action, and even a military arm in the "Minutemen." Fred Koch, of the Koch Brothers industries that remain major "small government" and "free market" funders, was a founding member of the John Birch Society.

This highly public reassertion of white supremacy and the Birch Society's methods of founding activist local chapters to take over school boards and other local offices across the country became a hallmark of the new right movement, embraced by the transformed National Rifle Association in the 1970s, coinciding with the rising visibility and politicization of the right-wing evangelical movement. The first time the movement revealed its collective power was in support of Barry Goldwater's candidacy in 1964.[18] Goldwater didn't make it, but the movement grew, so that in California, the avatar of the new right, Ronald Reagan, was elected governor for two terms, serving from 1966 to 72, then became president of the United States in 1980.

During the period 1954–64, following the use of nuclear weapons against Japan and a stalemated proxy war between the U.S. and the People's Republic of China in Korea, national liberation movements arose in Africa, Asia, Latin America, and the Caribbean, most succeeding in evicting French, Belgian, Dutch, Portuguese, and British colonizers from their countries. While these movements inspired activist African Americans, Puerto Ricans, Indigenous Peoples, Chicanos, and Asian Americans, as well as white anti-imperialist and anti-war activists and students, they had the opposite effect on those who feared the loss of white supremacy in the United States and the loss of U.S. supremacy in the world, and among the elite, who feared loss of confidence in capitalism.

The National Rifle Association was one of the formations transformed during this period of right-wing growth. Up to 1975, the N.R.A. had not opposed gun regulations and had not made a fetish of the Second Amendment. It had been founded following the Civil War by a group of former

Union Army officers in the North to sponsor marksmanship training and competitions. Since the late nineteenth century, target shooting has been a part of the Olympics. In 1934, during the Depression, the N.R.A. testified in favor of the first federal gun legislation that sought to keep machine guns away from outlaws, such as the famous Bonnie and Clyde and Pretty Boy Floyd, and Chicago gangsters. During testimony, a Congressman asked the N.R.A. witness if the proposed law would violate the Constitution, the witness said he knew of none. When the N.R.A. opened a new headquarters in the late 1950s, its marquee advertised firearms safety education, marksmanship training, and recreational shooting (hunting).

By the time of its 1977 convention, the Second Amendment Foundation and its lobbying arm, the Citizens Committee for the Right to Keep and Bear Arms, founded in Washington State in 1974 seized leadership of the N.R.A. It was then that the N.R.A. centered the Second Amendment as its main concern.[19] Harlon Carter was the primary actor in this "coup" that transformed the N.R.A. Carter, following the career path of his father, had been a U.S. Border Patrol chief with a checkered past. As a youth he killed a fellow teenager, who was Mexican, and was sentenced to three years in prison, which was overturned soon after. As a U.S. Border Patrol chief, Carter was head of the mid-1950s "Operation Wetback" program, a violent, corrupt, and massive roundup and deportation of people who were allegedly undocumented Mexicans. Journalist and author Mark Ames writes:

The seemingly strange amalgam that Harlon represents—pro-gun, pro–border guard, violent fear of dark southern immigrants, combined with a fear and hatred of the federal government—is still around today, the basic material of Ron and Rand Paul, both of whom have some crazy extreme ideas about massively militarizing the southern border and making citizenship harder to achieve, while at the same time railing against the federal government, and pushing for a culture in which every home is packed full of firearms.[20]

N.R.A. membership numbers soared during the early years of the Reagan White House. As California governor, Reagan had indulged the John Birch Society, which helped him win the California governorship in 1966; then in 1980, as a presidential candidate, he promised to implement Harlon Carter's N.R.A. pro-gun agenda as soon as he took office. As for Carter, by the mid-1980s, gun cultists even more fanatic than he was threw him out of leadership. That trend continues today. As Ames puts it, "The formula is simple: The more batshit malevolent the gun cult gets, the more power they exert. Just ignore the periodic squeals from the rest of the country, and keep pushing the batshit envelope. There is power in acting like the crazy one who needs to be talked down, so long as you convincingly mean it."[21]

The large N.R.A. headquarters in Fairfax, Virginia, has the Second Amendment written on the lobby wall, but only the second part: "The right of the people to keep and Bear Arms, shall not be infringed."

In April 2017, in Atlanta, President Donald Trump addressed the enthralled N.R.A. membership gathered at its annual convention: "Only one candidate in the general election came to speak to you, and that candidate is now the president of the United States, standing before you. . . . You came through for me, and I am going to come through for you."[22] Trump had spoken at the N.R.A. convention in Nashville in April 2016, before winning the Republican primaries. Ironically, gun sales had been plummeting ever since President Obama left office. George Zornick writes on the N.R.A in a feature story for *The Nation*:

> The Obama administration provided an eight-year sugar high for the industry, with imagined fears of a nationwide gun-confiscation program fueling sales. Particularly after the Sandy Hook massacre in Newtown, Connecticut, in 2012, industry profits boomed: There were 19 straight months of increased year over year sales, according to FBI background-check data. (There is no public tracking of gun sales nationwide.) But as soon as Trump was elected, stock prices for the major gun companies plummeted, and they haven't fully recovered. In April, a full third of the outstanding shares in Sturm Ruger, for example, are short bets.
>
> "In the firearms segment, we've experienced the expected slowdown in demand for modern sporting-rifle products and handguns post the presidential election," said Steve Jackson, chief financial officer of the Remington Outdoor Company,

which now owns some of the biggest gun manufacturers in the country. Speaking to investors in an early April conference call, Jackson noted that inventory levels were problematically high, because "retailers and wholesalers expected a different political climate and hunting season that did not materialize." Most of the publicly traded firearm companies reported similar situations in their first-quarter reports for this year.[23]

The more that gun-control advocates raise the issue of government regulation, particularly federal government regulation, the more ammunition is provided to those who hold the Second Amendment sacred to stand their ground. And because gun-control advocates erroneously misinterpret the Second Amendment provisions as being related only to the individual right to hunt and to militias as national guards, they delude themselves, failing to comprehend the history embedded in contemporary U.S. culture and social relations. The Constitution is the sacred text of the civic religion that is U.S. nationalism, and that nationalism is inexorably tied to white supremacy.

SEVEN

MASS SHOOTINGS

"Such is the commemorative sleight of hand that renders a raid resulting in four deaths more objectionable than a day's battle costing thousands of lives," writes historian Matthew Christopher Hulbert, regarding Confederate guerrillas' actions in the Civil War compared to the massive slaughter of the two national armies.[1] This observation could be rephrased to make the point about the horror expressed about mass shootings in light of U.S. wars for the past half-century.

Similar outrage could be expressed over gang shootings from the 1980s and 1990s in Los Angeles to South Chicago in the new millennium compared to U.S.-sponsored death squads, coups, counterinsurgencies, and wars taking place at the same time. In 1991, after the Los Angeles uprising protesting the acquittal of LAPD officers in the videotaped beating of Rodney King, when asked about "drive-by shootings" by Crips and Bloods, a gang leader responded, "What about those fly-by shootings in Iraq?" It was a fair question a few months after Operation Desert Storm's devastating 24/7 bombing of Baghdad, with 88,500 tons of bombs dropped in thirty-seven days during which time countless people were slaughtered.

Mass shootings have no direct relationship with the Second Amendment, but have everything to do with the demands for stricter gun regulations and the banning of AR-15, as well as the N.R.A.'s argument for gun rights based on the Second Amendment. These catastrophic events occur more frequently in the United States than in other countries, but only account for a tiny percentage of U.S. gun-related deaths.

There is no way to prove a correlation between war crimes—the U.S. bombing of civilian populations and their infrastructure—and domestic mass shootings, but the relationship does not appear to be random. The definition of "mass shootings" varies, but is generally defined by four or more deaths in one location by a lone gunman, or in a few cases, such as Columbine and San Bernardino, two. There were 128 such events with 932 victims in the United States between 1966 and late 2017, with an average of seven deaths in each. Only three of the 131 shooters were women.[2] However, if domestic shootings are included, meaning a man shooting his partner, often including their children and other relatives, the occurrence rises dramatically. A *New York Times* report titled "How Often Do Mass Shootings Occur? On Average, Every Day, Records Show" uses the measure of four or more wounded, and includes domestic shootings. More than two-thirds took place in private residences and included "a current or former intimate partner or family member of the attacker. Half of all victims were women.[3] Investigative journalist Jane Mayer further links domestic violence and many non-domestic mass shootings. Shortly after the June 2017 shooting that wounded House Majority Whip Steve Scalise and four others, it was known that the shooter James Hodgkinson had a history of domestic violence. The shooter in the 2015 Planned Parenthood Clinic had an arrest record of rape and sexual violence. Mayer writes, "In the meantime, many domestic-violence suspects, like Hodgkinson, are arrested only to have the charges dropped later, which leaves them armed and dangerous. The National Rifle Association and its allies have successfully argued that a mere arrest on domestic-violence charges . . . is not sufficient reason to deprive a citizen of his right to bear arms."[4] Some mass shootings have taken aim at women simply because they are women. Also, women are wounded or killed by their partners by stabbing, slashing, punching, strangling, stomping, kicking, running over, beating with various objects, and other means more frequently than with guns, but the gun nearly always guarantees death.

The history of public mass shootings by a lone gunman killing or wounding strangers is important to trace, as they parallel the rise of the gun-rights movement and ramped-up militarism. This suggests that it is not only the sheer number of guns in the hands of private citizens or the lack of regulation and licensing, but also a gun culture at work, along with a military culture, matters more difficult to resolve than by imposing regulations on firearms.

The first notable mass shooting, in 1966, is often not counted, because there were no more of that character until 1982, when they began with some regularity. But the University of Texas mass shooting is significant and in retrospect was no anomaly, more like a comet that would return. Former Marine sniper and UT engineering student Charles Whitman shot and killed fourteen people and wounded another thirty-two while perched for ninety minutes on top of the twenty-seven-story Clock Tower on the University of Texas, Austin, campus, before he was killed by police. Early that morning, he had strangled his mother to death and murdered his wife by stabbing her in the heart as she slept. He later explained that he didn't want them to be ashamed of him and suffer for his actions. Whitman had been in the Marine Corps, but did not serve in combat and completed his service before U.S. troops were deployed to Vietnam. However, he had suffered a head injury from a jeep accident during his service. Whitman kept a detailed journal in the months before the shootings, recording his severe headaches and feelings of rage, his failure to get help from multiple doctors he consulted, and the ineffectiveness of the medications they prescribed. In the autopsy of his body, doctors discovered a pecan-size tumor in his brain that could have caused his derangement. In the wake of the tragedy, rather than taking action to improve preventive health care at the university or the state, authorities created the first S.W.A.T. team, soon to be replicated in nearly every police force in the country.[5]

In January 2016, a new Texas law went into effect allowing handgun permit holders, who had been required to conceal their weapons, to carry handguns openly, except on public or private university or college campuses; then, on August 1, 2016, on the fiftieth anniversary of the University of Texas Tower shooting massacre, the legislature included public university campuses among the locales where people have the right to openly carry handguns. Also, the Texas handgun license is equal to a driver's license as official identification for security checks, voting, or any other request for identification. In an article titled: "America's Future is Texas," author Lawrence Wright observes: "An eccentric feature of Texas's new gun laws is that people entering the state capitol can skip the long lines of tourists waiting to pass through metal detectors if they show guards a license-to-carry permit. In other words, the people most likely to bring weapons into the building aren't scanned at all. Many of the people who breeze through are lawmakers and staffers who tote concealed weapons into offices or onto the floor of the legislature. But some lobbyists and reporters have also obtained gun licenses, just to skirt the lines. I recently got one myself."[6]

Wright, a Texan himself, also writes: "Especially among Texas politicians, there's a locker-room lust for weaponry that belies noble-sounding proclamations about self-protection and Second Amendment rights. In 2010, Governor Perry boasted of killing with a single shot a coyote that was menacing his daughter's Labrador. Perry was jogging at the time, but naturally he was packing heat: a .380 Ruger. The gun's manufacturer promptly issued a Coyote Special edition of the gun, which comes in a box labelled 'for sale to Texans only.'"[7]

The University of Texas massacre took place at the height of the war in Southeast Asia, which was televised nationwide daily. Yet the public reaction of horror and shock at the mass shooting was far more intense than reactions to the U.S. soldiers slaughtering villagers in Vietnam on the nightly news. And so the trend continued, when mass shootings resumed sixteen years later during the Reagan administration.

Nearly 30 percent of all mass shootings that have resulted in multiple deaths have occurred in workplaces, usually by an angry former employee. The first workplace shooting with a large death toll took place in Edmond, Oklahoma, a small college town north of Oklahoma City. In August 1986, a forty-four year old former Marine and part-time U.S. Postal Service worker, after receiving a negative work review, stormed into the town's small, busy post office. Dressed as if for work in his mail carrier's uniform and carrying three handguns in his mailbag, he killed fourteen and wounded six before shooting himself. In the decade before, there had been five other post office shootings by former or current workers, with one or two fatalities. More followed almost annually, giving rise in the early 1990s to the grim term "going postal." Dozens of other workplace shootings have taken place—in office buildings, strip malls, factories, night clubs, restaurants, military bases, and universities (employee related, unlike the separate category of "school shootings" targeting students) during the time period of mass shootings from the late 1980s on.

Two mass shootings in restaurants do not conform to the "workplace shooting" rubric, each with the highest body count up to the 2007 Virginia Tech massacre. Neither shooter had been employed or knew anyone in the restaurants. Both were likely hate crimes, targeting Mexicans in one case and women in the other.

The mass shooting at a McDonald's in San Ysidro, California, in 1984 was the largest up to that time, with twenty-two left dead, including the shooter, and nineteen wounded; one of the victims was pregnant, and another victim was an eight-month-old baby. San Ysidro is inside the United States on the border across from Tijuana, Mexico, but people of Mexican descent comprise 90 percent of its population. Nearly all the shooting victims were of Mexican descent. The shooter, a forty-one-year-old Anglo-American, was armed with a shotgun and an Uzi. After seventy-eight minutes of the gunman's killing spree, firing at least 245 rounds, a S.W.A.T. team moved in and shot him. James Oliver Huberty, the shooter, was born and lived most of his life in Ohio, a serial failure at starting a business, but moved to Tijuana, then San Ysidro a year before the massacre. Back in Ohio, he had been a dedicated survivalist, apparently not with an organized group; he accumulated an arsenal and also hoarded food and other survival necessities, taking it all along in the move west. He believed government regulations caused his business failures and that international bankers controlled the Federal Reserve, with communist dominance everywhere, economic collapse and nuclear war imminent.[8] These were the Reagan years.

The next largest mass shooting after San Ysidro occurred on October 16, 1991, and also took place in a restaurant, Luby's Cafeteria in Killeen, Texas. The shooter was not tied to the restaurant in any way. Killeen was a town of around 64,000 people in 1991, and also host to the enormous Ft. Hood Army base (named after Confederate general John Bell Hood in 1942). Thirty-five-year-old civilian

George Jo Hennard drove his pickup truck into the plate glass window of Luby's while some 150 patrons were having dinner. Armed with a Glock 17 and a Ruger P89, he then jumped out of his vehicle and into the restaurant yelling, "All women of Killeen and Belton are vipers!"⁹ Then he began shooting, killing twenty-three, fourteen of them women, whom he appeared to be targeting, yelling "Bitch!" as he shot. The violence ended when he shot himself. In the days after, those who had worked or lived with him told reporters that he hated women, as well as gay people, African Americans, and Mexicans. Some days before his rampage, Hennard is reported to have expressed rage in a restaurant while watching television coverage of Anita Hill's testimony accusing Clarence Thomas, candidate for the Supreme Court, of sexual harassment. The restaurant manager said: "When an interview with Anita Hill came on, he just went off. He started screaming at the television, 'You dumb bitch! You bastards opened the door for all the women!'"¹⁰

Thirteen percent of mass shootings have occurred in schools. Not the first, but the most shocking one up to that time was the 1999 Columbine High School shootings by students Eric Harris and Dylan Klebold that took thirteen lives—twelve students and a teacher. The apparently normal upper-middle-class families of the two high school students seemed an unlikely background to produce such violence under their parents' noses without their noticing anything awry about their sons. The shooting rampage inside the school took place over several hours, while most students escaped. Only after the sound of gunfire ceased did police storm the building, where they found the two killers had shot themselves.[11]

Certainly there had been many shootings in schools from the early 1800s to the 1966 Texas Tower massacre, but none had been mass shootings with multiple victims. There were dozens of school shooting incidents between the 1966 UT tower shooting and 1989, but they began to occur with troubling frequency and more deadly outcomes in the 1990s, culminating in Columbine at the end of the millennium. After 2000, the number of school shootings increased from single digits to double digits by 2005, with three catastrophic ones, none of which fit the alleged "patterns" that had been theorized—mainly about possible reactions to bullying—bringing into question the notion that any of them did.

None was more baffling and tragic than the December 2012 mass shooting at the elementary school in Newton, Connecticut, where twenty-year-old Adam Lanza slaughtered twenty first-graders, along with six adult school personnel, before ending his own life. Children and babies had been killed in past mass shootings,[12] but not specifically targeted as at Sandy Hook. Earlier, Lanza had shot and killed his mother while she slept in the home they shared. The mother, Nancy Lanza, was a gun hoarder and avid recreational shooter. Because her son suffered Asperger's syndrome, he was mostly home-schooled and had little social life, and she found that he enjoyed going with her to the shooting range, which she apparently considered appropriate therapy. She obviously had no fear of possible violence from the son, as she kept her multiple high-powered firearms and ammunition in the house where they both lived.

At the height of the U.S. military and mercenary killing in Iraq, in March 2005, conjuring memories of nineteenth-century wars against Native peoples, a sixteen-year old Anishinaabe citizen created his own war in the Red Lake Nation, located in the far north of what is today the state of Minnesota. Jeffrey Weise killed his beloved grandfather (a tribal police officer) and his grandfather's girlfriend at their home. After taking his grandfather's police weapons and bulletproof vest, Weise drove his grandfather's police vehicle to Red Lake Senior High School, where he had dropped out of school some months before. Weise shot and killed seven people at the school and wounded five others. The dead included an unarmed security guard at the entrance of the school, a teacher, and five students. After the police arrived, Weise exchanged gunfire with them. He was wounded and then committed suicide in a vacant classroom. Young Jeffrey had been interacting online with various neo-Nazi and other violent right-wing groups.[13]

On April 16, 2007, a new record was set for mass shootings, with thirty-two dead and twenty-three wounded on the Virginia Tech University campus in Blacksburg, Virginia. The shooter was twenty-three-year-old senior Seung-Hui Cho, using Glock 19 and Walther P22 pistols and stocked with four hundred rounds of ammunition. The other national news coming from Virginia that spring was eclipsed by the shooting—an eighteen-month celebration of the founding of the first British colony of the thirteen that would be formed over the next 125 years. During the month of April 2007, leading up to the May 3 visit of Queen Elizabeth to Jamestown for the celebrations, there was daily news coverage locally and nationally of the plans and special programming on the history of Jamestown. Some descendants of the Powhatan people whose land was taken for the settlement were on hand to provide entertainment, but there was no mention, much less apologies, for the murder of Powhatan farmers and the destruction of their homes and fields that accompanied British "settlement." And in the days after the Virginia Tech shootings, no mention was made of what had happened at Jamestown four centuries earlier. One could speculate that the shooter, Cho, may have taken note. Jamestown was famously the first permanent settlement that gave birth to the Commonwealth of Virginia, the colonial epicenter of what became the United States of America nearly two centuries later, the colony out of which was carved the U.S. capital, Washington, on the river that met the sea up the coast. A few years after Jamestown was established, the more familiar and revered colony of Plymouth was implanted by English religious dissidents, under the auspices of private investors with royal approval, as with Jamestown, and engaging in the same mercenary activities personified by Captain John Smith. This was the beginning of British overseas colonialism, after the conquest and colonization of Scotland, Wales, and Ireland turned England into Great Britain.

The Virginia Tech shootings were described in 2007 as the "worst mass killing," the "worst massacre," in U.S. history. Descendants of massacred Indigenous ancestors took exception to that designation. Lakota Joan Redfern expressed the reaction of many, saying, "To say the Virginia shooting is the worst in all of U.S. history is to pour salt on old wounds. It means erasing and forgetting all of our ancestors who were killed in the past."[14]

It was curious with the media circus surrounding the Jamestown celebration, and with Queen Elizabeth and President George W. Bush presiding, that journalists failed to compare the colonial massacres of Powhatans four centuries earlier and the single, disturbed individual's shootings of his classmates. The shooter himself, born in South Korea and brought to the United States by his parents at age eight, was a child of colonial war, the U.S. war in Korea and continued presence of tens of thousands of heavily armed U.S. troops. He had been diagnosed as depressed but was likely bipolar. He appeared to be overwhelmed by wealthy, white students, who made up 75 percent of the undergraduate student body. In the videotaped manifesto Cho made and sent to the press before his rampage, he called his fellow students "sadistic snobs," and said further: "You have never felt a single ounce of pain your whole life. Did you want to inject as much misery in our lives as you can just because you can? You had everything you wanted. Your Mercedes wasn't enough, you brats. Your golden necklaces weren't enough, you snobs. Your trust fund wasn't enough. Your Vodka and Cognac weren't enough. All your debaucheries weren't enough. Those weren't enough to fulfill your hedonistic needs. You had everything."[15]

Then there was Orlando. Outdoing all the mass shootings of this type that had preceded it: forty-nine dead and fifty-three wounded. The shooter, Omar Mateen, a twenty-nine-year-old U.S. citizen of Afghani Pashtun descent, used a SIG MCX semiautomatic rifle and a 9mm Glock 17. Like

Cho, he was at war with his peers. His victims were from the GLBTQ community, and most of the fatalities that night were of Puerto Rican descent; it was Latino night at the Pulse gay nightclub on June 12, 2016. Mateen had frequented the club. This was the second mass shooting of civilians directly associated with ongoing U.S. wars. Mateen, a Sunni Muslim, had sworn loyalty to the Islamic State of Iraq and Syria ISIS), the most recent terrorist jihadist group to rise out of U.S. wars in the Middle East. Six months earlier, Syed Rizwan Farook and Tashfeen Malik, a married couple who were legal immigrants from Pakistan, interrupted a holiday party at the Inland Regional Center in San Bernardino, where Mr. Farook was an employee. They pulled out automatic weapons, firing randomly it appeared, killing fourteen and injuring twenty-two. Quickly, the FBI traced the terror attack back to before their immigration to the United States and their allegiance to the Islamic State terror organization that the United States is at war with in Iraq.

On Sunday evening, October 1, 2017, records were temporarily broken for the number of people killed during a mass shooting perpetrated by a single gunman. On that occasion, sixty-four-year-old Stephen Craig Paddock shot to death fifty-nine people, including himself, with nearly five hundred hospitalized with injuries resulting from the incident. Paddock was born in Iowa and had lived in Florida, Texas, and an upscale retirement community in Mesquite, Nevada, near the Arizona and Utah borders. Four days prior to his massacre-suicide, Paddock checked into a 32nd-floor suite at the luxury casino-hotel Mandalay in Las Vegas. Having been a high-rolling professional gambler at the hotel for some time, Paddock was familiar to the staff, who comped him the expensive suite as a perk for gambling on their premises.

Under the lax scrutiny of "what happens in Vegas stays in Vegas," Paddock managed to stockpile his room with twenty-two high-powered scoped rifles ranging in size from .308 to .223 caliber, two tripods, and thousands of rounds of ammunition. Just after 10:00 p.m. that Sunday night, Paddock broke two windows in the suite and began firing semi-automatic weapons that had been fitted with a "bump stock" device that allowed him to increase the speed he could fire bullets into the crowd. His target was a packed, shoulder-to-shoulder crowd of 22,000 people enjoying the final set of a country music festival taking place in the open air across from his hotel. Paddock attacked the audience with ten long minutes of non-stop shooting.

Paddock owned multiple properties in Nevada, where police found more weapons, approximately fifty in all, half of which Paddock had purchased during the previous twelve months in Nevada, Utah, Arizona, and California. Every weapon and device Paddock owned was legal and registered under his name, including the "bump stock." For gun enthusiasts and those familiar with them, the number of weapons Paddock possessed was far from shocking.[16]

During the days following the mass murder in Las Vegas, the N.R.A. and Republican leadership, as well as President Donald Trump, cautioned those who immediately demanded gun control legislation not to "politicize" the tragic event during a time of mourning. Yet, on October 5, 2017, in an unprecedented move since its extreme radicalization, the N.R.A. announced its support for the Bureau of Alcohol, Tobacco, and Firearms to consider firearms regulation: "The N.R.A. believes that devices designed to allow semiautomatic rifles to function like fully-automatic rifles should be subject to additional regulations."[17]

Meditating on five major undeclared wars perpetrated by the U.S. since World War II—Korea, Vietnam, Central America (1981–89), Iraq (1991; 2003, continuing) and Afghanistan (1979–89; 2001, continuing) and not counting the dozens of brutal interventions and coups in Latin America, the Caribbean, Africa, and Asia—with flashes of historical memory of Jamestown, the Ohio Valley, and Wounded Knee, brings us to the essence of U.S. history. A red thread of blood connects the first white settlement in North America with today and the future. As military historian John Grenier puts it: "U.S. people are taught that their military culture does not approve of or encourage targeting and killing civilians and know little or nothing about the nearly three centuries of warfare—before and after the founding of the U.S.—that reduced the Indigenous peoples of the continent to a few reservations by burning their towns and fields and killing civilians, driving the refugees out—step by step—across the continent. . . . Violence directed systematically against noncombatants through irregular means, from the start, has been a central part of Americans' way of war."[18]

Just why these events, horrific as they are, and tragic for the families and communities traumatized by senseless violence and loss, loom so large in the public mind is a mystery, when, during the entire period since the 1966 Whitman massacre, the United States has perpetrated massive amounts of violence around the world, responsible for killing millions of people and families. Rather than the interpretation that mass shootings, gun hoarding, and popularity of military-style firearms among civilians are a product of the gun lobby or the gun industry, it may be more clearly framed as a domestic expression of "the new American militarism."[19] Military historian and retired Army Colonel Andrew J. Bacevich, who is also a West Point graduate and veteran of the Vietnam and 1991 Gulf Wars, does not make that connection in his important book by that title, but he does see the rise in militarism and endless wars as a backlash to the U.S. military defeat in Vietnam, in which he was an Army officer. It could be added that the defense contracting corporations that had profited mightily during the decade of war in Southeast Asia played a significant role in bringing Ronald Reagan to the White House, and that this industry escaped deindustrialization and relocation while many others moved their operations off shore.

Concerted attention to mass shootings has increased since the 2001 bombings of the Pentagon and the World Trade Center towers, followed by the U.S. wars in Afghanistan and Iraq, which continue to this day. It may be that the mass killings at home are easier to grasp, condemn, and mourn than those perpetrated as military operations in the name of the people of the United States, paid for with their taxes, and soldiered by their children. Thus we had prominent Democratic Party officials, including Barack Obama in an eight-year presidency, urgently calling for gun regulations and banning some weapons in the United States, while fully supporting the unlimited production of bombs, bombers, and drones to kill people on a daily basis. And it only got worse in 2017, when the new president, Donald J. Trump, proposed an $18 billion increase in the Defense Department budget, only to be outdone by Republican Congress members, who drew up a 2018 budget that increased defense spending $37 billion more, totaling $640 billion.[20]

Since 1990, there has been no serious political effort to reduce the Defense Department budget; yet, in response to mass shootings, no money can be found to finance mental health facilities, mental health problems being the one attribute that nearly all the mass shooters share. Nor is it suggested by advocates of gun control or even mental health specialists that mass shootings, invariably carried out by mentally troubled individuals, may be related to the actual killing, bombing, and warfare the country has engaged in since 1965.

British journalist Ian Overton's assessment of international arms transfers can be found in his 2016 book *The Way of the Gun: A Bloody Journey into the World of Firearms.*[21] Overton heads a nonprofit organization in London, Action on Armed Violence, to research and lobby against the proliferation of firearms and gun violence against civilians all over the world. There are nearly a billion firearms worldwide, many more than ever before, in large part due to U.S. wars in the early twenty-first century. However, more than a hundred countries have their own gun manufacturers, and Overton did not expect his project to focus on the United States. When he began, his research and focus were particularly concerned with gun proliferation and violence in less developed countries, but he realized that most media information related to the United States. In part he blames the media for focusing on the superpower: "But it is also because the U.S. has, quite simply, the most unique relationship with guns of any other country I know."[22] He also traces the source of the world's burgeoning acquisition of firearms to Pentagon sales and use. Using the U.S. Freedom of Information Act, Overton collected fourteen years of Pentagon contract information, 412 contracts in all, concerning firearms for U.S. soldiers, as well as for their proxies and allies. He found that the Pentagon provided more than 1.45 million firearms to various security forces in Afghanistan and Iraq, including more than 978,000 assault rifles, 266,000 pistols, and almost 112,000 machine guns. These transfers included all types of firearms—AK-47s left over from the Cold War, newer NATO-standard M16s and M4s, sniper rifles, shotguns and various kinds and calibers of pistols, including a large order of Glock semiautomatic pistols.

The United States is also the largest exporter of military weapons in the world, totaling nearly $40 billion in sales in 2014, far greater than the second-biggest weapons dealer, France, at $15 billion.[23] The Stockholm International Peace Research Institute (SIPRI) reported in February 2017 that transfers of major weapons had reached their highest volume for any five-year period since the end of the Cold War. Of the Earth's ten top weapons manufacturing companies, seven are in the United States: Boeing, Raytheon, Northrop Grumman, General Dynamic, and United

Technologies, together employing nearly 800,000 workers. Thirty-five other U.S. corporations also manufacture weapons, including General Electric, better known for electrical appliances, and Hewlett-Packard, which specializes in consumer electronics.[24]

The International Arms Trade Treaty took effect in 2014, with the United States as a signatory.[25] Its mandate is modest—to promote and monitor transparency and responsible action in the transfer of arms, including preventing losing track of them. Those who support firearms control, especially lawmakers, should support implementation of the terms of this treaty. It is possible that education about the treaty could have an effect on gun proliferation and violence within the U.S. while raising questions about the Americanism of the Second Amendment and the violent racist legacies of colonial-derived militarism.

EIGHT

WHITE NATIONALISM, THE MILITIA MOVEMENT, AND TEA PARTY PATRIOTS

On Wednesday evening, June 17, 2015, perhaps the most historically symbolic, specifically targeted, and racially motivated U.S. mass shooting took place in Charleston, South Carolina. The site of the slaughter of nine people was a church. For evangelical Protestant congregations in the United States, Wednesday evening is prayer meeting and Bible reading in gatherings of the most dedicatedly faithful. But this was a very specific Protestant Church that was targeted, the Emanuel African Methodist Episcopal (AME) Church of Charleston—"Mother Emanuel"—the oldest historically Black church in North America, also a historical site of slave resistance, being the church co-founded by Denmark Vesey.

Denmark Vesey was born into slavery in 1767, but at age thirty-two in 1799, he won a lottery and purchased his freedom. He never was able to raise enough money to purchase the freedom of his wife and two sons. Vesey was literate and a skilled carpenter who operated his own business. In 1818, he co-founded Emanuel AME church, which quickly attracted nearly a thousand members. Vesey was free, and respected by his white clients and white clergymen. But Vesey also continued to identify and socialize with those who remained in bondage, including his own family. In 1819, as Congress debated whether slavery would be permitted in the new state of Missouri, Vesey may have had hope that the end of legalized slavery was on the horizon, but the decision went the other way, and the 1820 Missouri Constitution allowed white settlers to buy, sell, and own enslaved Africans. It is not known if this disappointment led Vesey to organize a revolt, or, more likely, it had been longer in the planning. The Haitian Revolution, 1791–1804, carried out by enslaved Africans, ended in national independence and the abolition of slavery, which struck fear in U.S. American slavers and inspiration in Black people—free and enslaved—throughout the hemisphere. Over a period of time, Vesey secretly organized enslaved and free Africans, borrowing from the Haitian revolution's strategy. At the time of the planned revolt, 25,000 people lived in Charleston, only 11,000 of whom were white. Before the date set for the uprising—June 16, 1822—slavers learned about the plan and immediately mobilized all the armed white citizens, arresting Vesey and dozens of others. Vesey and five enslaved Africans were hanged on July 2, 1822. One of Vesey's still-enslaved sons was arrested and deported to the Caribbean; his other enslaved son, Robert, survived to be emancipated during the Civil War and helped rebuild the war-damaged AME church his father had co-founded.

Later explaining that he sought to ignite a race war by his vile deed, twenty-one-year-old Dylann Roof, who is white, arrived at the Wednesday prayer meeting and was welcomed by the twelve African-American attendees, including the nationally and internationally known and respected AME senior pastor, who was also a South Carolina state senator, Clementa C. Pinckney. After an hour of Bible study, Roof pulled out a Glock 41 and a .45 caliber pistol, both loaded with hollow-point bullets,[1] reloading five times, killing all but three people present. He may have been expecting a larger attendance as he was carrying eight magazines filled with bullets. Roof fled the bloody scene and was later apprehended and arrested. The date Roof had chosen to hatch his plan was obviously premeditated—it was the 193rd anniversary of the Vesey-led revolt.

Images circulated on social media quickly made clear that Roof was a white nationalist. First there was his manifesto—loaded with slurs on African Americans, Jews, Latinos, and Asians—that claimed he had become "racially aware" following the shooting of Trayvon Martin in 2012. He said that while searching the web to learn about the case, he concluded that the killer, George Zimmerman, was right; what convinced him was the information he came upon at white nationalist websites and chat rooms. One picture on Roof's website showed him wearing a jacket with two white nationalist symbols sewed into the fabric—the flag of the former apartheid South African state and the flag of the former white Rhodesia Republic (before it was overthrown by the Zimbabwe liberation movements in 1980). Roof even had a website registered under his name that he called "The

Last Rhodesian." What stood out for most of those who had never even heard of Rhodesia, was the picture of him posing with a pistol and a Confederate Battle Flag.

The widespread attention given to Roof's Confederate affinity and espousal of white nationalism, which he had made no secret about, together with the growing presence of white nationalists during the following months at Donald J. Trump stadium rallies, thrust the topic of white supremacy out in the open nationwide. Such exposure drove home the fact that most of those who propagate white nationalism were not mentally ill, but rather ideologically driven, and way beyond the Confederate Battle Flag, the Lost Cause, or limited to the South, although those tropes remained integral to the anti-Black and anti-Mexican racism that are at the core of present-day white nationalism in the United States.

This became clear as Trump installed white nationalists and military men as his closest advisers and cabinet appointees, and continued to hold rallies where he demonized Muslims and Mexicans. A new breed of white nationalists, self-identifying as "alt-right" and fed through online commercial operations like *Breitbart News*, began supporting insurgent "Trumpist" politicians to destabilize "establishment Republicans."

Since the issue of Confederate statuary received nation-wide attention following the Charleston, South Carolina, massacre by a self-proclaimed Confederate-loving fascist, members of the alt-right joined forces with neo-Nazis, Lost Cause Confederate fetishists, including the KKK, to storm the University of Virginia campus in support of maintaining the prominent monument to Robert E. Lee, the Confederate general of Confederate Virginia. In the opening gesture of their "Unite the Right" weekend rally, they marched to the Robert E. Lee monument bearing tiki torches, chanting, "You will not replace us" and "One People, one nation, end immigration," many giving the Nazi salute. University students, local anti-racist activists, and Black and white clergy who organized a huge presence to oppose the racist gather-ing were attacked by the intruders, and on Sunday, one of the self-identified fascists plowed his car at high speed into a group of locals demonstrating against the rally, killing thirty-two-year-old Heather Heyer, a well-loved member of the Charlottesville community. President Trump refused to hold the fascists accountable for the melee, injuries, and killing, saying "both sides" were to blame.[2]

A strong anti-fascist movement developed in the late 1980s and 1990s to oppose the resurgence of racist intolerance and fascist violence. The movement was already three decades old when it sprang to oppose the aggressive spread of pro-fascist forces coinciding with the rise of Donald Trump, former White House adviser Steve Bannon, and Trumpism.[3]

As suggested earlier, the rise and institutionalization of the Ronald Reagan political clique, first in California as governor, 1967–75, and then as U.S. president, 1981–1989, a major green light for the development of white supremacist groups, from marginal and obscure to mainstream, by the dawn of the twenty-first century. Reagan and his cronies and political descendants were masters of the device that came to be known as a "dog whistle," using certain tropes and symbolic actions that telegraphed toxic white supremacy and anti-Black racism. As Reagan's "free market" economic and anti-union policies, accompanied by rapid de-industrialization and job shrinkage, produced homelessness and insecurity of the most vulnerable, they also increasingly affected white workers, making them easy prey to the white nationalist and politicized evangelical groups that had their own narrative about the causes—big government (including mysterious black helicopters), secularization, banks (always implicating Jews), poverty programs (always identified with African Americans even though the majority of recipients were in fact white), and Mexican migrants and women taking their jobs.

One example that broadcast Reagan's racist agenda took place three months before the 1980 presidential election, when Reagan chose the significant date of August 3 to give a campaign speech extolling "states rights" near the town of Philadelphia, Mississippi, at the Neshoba Country Fair in Neshoba County. There, on June 21, 1964, three organizers for the Congress of Racial Equality, one being a local African American, the other two northern Jewish young men—James Chaney, Andrew Goodman, and Michael Schwerner—had been abducted by the local Ku Klux Klan with the cooperation of the Neshoba County Sheriff's Office and the Philadelphia Police Department. Their bodies, riddled with bullets, were found buried in a dam near Philadelphia on August 3, 1964, sixteen years to the day before Reagan's speech on states-rights, another trope for segregation. Donald Trump Jr., campaigning for his father in the 2016 presidential campaign, also spoke at the Neshoba Country Fair, speaking to a crowd of two thousand:[4]

[Trump Jr.] drew large applause . . . when he said he is an avid outdoorsman and competition shooter and believes strongly in Second Amendment rights. The crowd also waved flags at his speech, mostly American, but with at least one large rebel flag and a "Don't Tread on Me" one. Trump Jr. before his speech was asked about the controversy at the Democratic National Convention over taking the Mississippi flag down because of its rebel canton. "I believe in tradition," Trump Jr. said. "I don't see a lot of the nonsense that's been created about that. I understand how some people feel but. . . . There's nothing wrong with some tradition."[5]

Anti-Semitism was integral to anti-Black racism for the Klan and newer Christian terrorist groups such as Richard G. Butler's Aryan Nations, which in 1976 began referring to the federal government as ZOG, that is, Zionist Occupation Government. These armed groups flourished and new ones sprouted, especially in the Pacific Northwest, where the Posse Comitatus group claimed in 1985 that "our nation is now completely under the control of the International Invisible government of World Jewry."[6] The Reagan administration signaled a thumbs-up to this movement three months into his second term in May 1985; on the fortieth anniversary of the end of World War II, the president visited the Bitburg cemetery, where dozens of Nazi Waffen SS men were buried.

At the same time, Reagan, as he had promised while campaigning, was intent on destroying the Soviet Union and all perceived communist governments or movements, communism also being attributed to Jews. This meant ramping up the possibility of nuclear war and led to mammoth increases in the Defense Department budget, all of which went to private Defense Department contractors and weapons manufacturers. Not only was military spending increased, but so too was militarization of the culture, as the Reagan-Bush administrations sought to destroy what they called the "Vietnam syndrome" of anti-war sentiment. There were also "dirty wars," clandestine operations with Reagan's "freedom fighters" against, among others around the globe, the governments of Nicaragua, Grenada, Angola, and Mozambique, and support for the apartheid regime in South Africa in fighting the liberation movements there and in Namibia. The largest CIA operation was in Afghanistan, where the Reagan administration armed Muslim fundamentalist jihadists with portable shoulder-to-air missiles and other weaponry to overthrow the elected government there, because of its friendly relations with its neighbor, the Soviet Union. This eight-year proxy war ended with Soviet withdrawal, leaving Afghanistan smashed, with millions of refugees and various warlords competing for power. It also led to the catastrophe of September 11, 2001, an action the Central Intelligence Agency immediately identified as "blowback" from those jihadists the United States had armed and empowered. Of course, the Reagan administration escalated the ongoing counterinsurgency and boycott of Cuba. While most Latin Americans were living under or escaping from brutal military and authoritarian regimes installed or sustained by the United States, peoples in the

Caribbean and Central America had ousted such governments in Nicaragua and Grenada in 1979, while the Socialist government of Michael Manley had won elections in Jamaica, all of which Reagan promised to reverse if elected. The Reagan administration also sent military advisers and mercenaries to support death-squad regimes in El Salvador and Guatemala in the attempt to wipe out leftist guerrillas, mass mobilizations, and political formations in those countries. Despite a sizable and widespread anti-war movement, the Reagan-Bush administrations realized their objectives, capped by the 1989 invasion and regime change in Panama and the 1991 invasion of Iraq.

But it was the Contra war against the leftist Sandinista (FSLN) government of Nicaragua that allowed a kind of populist "Wild West" scenario to develop, which brought the evangelical movement that had begun in the 1970s to own a war. While campaigning for president, Reagan had vowed to overthrow the "communistic" Sandinistas, and by the end of 1981, incursions by CIA-trained commandos into Nicaraguan territory had begun. The Reagan administration used the military-ruled friendly country of Honduras as the platform for training and arming several factions of anti-Sandinista Nicaraguans, principally the ousted Somoza's National Guard members. Under the leadership of evangelical celebrity preachers such as Pat Robertson, white evangelicals created a minor Christian Crusade that lasted for most of the 1980s, until the Sandinistas were voted out of power in 1989. The evangelicals delivered not only humanitarian assistance and Bibles, but also military surplus weapons—U.S. mercenaries and missionaries crawled all over the borderlands of Honduras and Nicaragua and mobilized their congregants at home. Militarization of U.S. culture was a rich setting for the organization of armed groups in the United States, loaded with conspiracy theories, a primary one being that liberals wanted to violate their sacred rights and confiscate their guns.[7]

In *Against the Fascist Creep*,[7] writer and activist Alexander Reid Ross traces the genealogy of the racist groups that descended from several sources during the Reagan era and gained momentum and followers in the 1990s with the advent of the Internet and social media, forming a key constituency of the Republican Party, and creating some cross-over affinity with a number of leftist and anarchist groups. Ross seeks to trace why and how "fascism"—under which rubric he includes white supremacists, anti-government militias, and other right-wing groups—"creeps into the mainstream and radical subcultures." Ross is also concerned that some left-leaning and particularly anarchist and libertarian individuals and groups incorporate right-wing populist ideas, often without realizing their source.[8]

The campaign of George Wallace (the former segregationist governor of Alabama) for president in 1968 mobilized many of the elements that would effect the radicalization of the N.R.A. as well as racist groups flourishing in the 1970s, especially a revived Ku Klux Klan. However, Louis Beam, the head of the Texas Klan, began promoting the ideology of "leaderless resistance," which was adopted by the Posse Comitatus. One of first visible actions based on that ideology took place in Arkansas in 1983, when tax resister and Posse Comitatus member Gordon Kahl refused to be served with a subpoena and instead started a gunfight, killing two marshals. He was pursued and shot dead by police, but became a martyr to the burgeoning movement. One of Beam's protégés in the Aryan Nations group, Robert Mathews, emulated the leaderless secret-cell concept in organizing a new white nationalist group, "The Order." The group raised millions of dollars by counterfeiting money and robbing banks and armored cars, using the proceeds to establish a network of safe houses all over the country and to fund other white nationalist groups. The Order collapsed with Matthews's death at the hands of the FBI after The Order, in 1984, assassinated Denver talk show host Alan Berg, who debated right-wing callers. The others involved in the network were rounded up and imprisoned, with one of their number, David Lane, becoming a celebrated white nationalist prisoner, his "14 Words" becoming sacred to neo-Nazis and other white nationalists. Those words are: "We must secure the existence of our people and a future for white children." The Feds put Beam and other leaders on trial and implicated still more, but only three were charged, and they were acquitted by jury trial.[9]

The Order was short-lived but inspiring to a later group calling themselves "Patriots," a movement that began the organization of what they called "sovereign citizens." Aryan Nation supporter Randy Weaver became the most famous of this movement. Weaver came from an evangelical Iowa farm family and was a Vietnam-era veteran stationed at Ft. Bragg for three years. Honorably discharged from the U.S. Army, he married in 1971 and enrolled at University of Northern Iowa to study criminal justice, hoping to become a FBI agent. He soon dropped out and took a job in the local John Deere factory. His wife, Vicki, raised evangelical, became increasingly fanatical in her belief in the impending end of the world.

In the early 1980s, the Weaver family bought a small, undeveloped property in a remote area of Idaho (near the town of Naples and the Ruby River), built a cabin, and home-schooled their children. In 1985, after attending some meetings of Aryan Nations, the couple was visited by the FBI and the Secret Service; they denied any affiliation. The FBI decided to try to recruit Weaver as an informer, a scheme that went awry with overlapping federal agencies working at odds with each other, and ended in Weaver being charged with possessing illegal weapons in January 1991. With some confusion in trial dates and Weaver not showing up, federal marshals attempted to arrest him at his remote home, where for ten days in August 1992, he and his family holed up and held off FBI snipers and some four hundred armed federal authorities. Vicki was shot and killed holding their ten-month-old baby; their fourteen-year-old son was shot and killed, as was the family dog; one federal marshal was also killed, and a wounded Randy Weaver surrendered, ending the siege. During the ten days, a crowd of assorted white nationalists and skinheads gathered outside the perimeter to support the Weavers, one prominent individual being Bo Gritz, the most highly decorated Green Beret in the Vietnam War, the real-life figure behind the Rambo character that Hollywood cashed in on and milked dry. Gritz was close to David Duke and a member of Willis Carto's Populist Party. Alexander Reid Ross writes: "Gritz was a symbol of veterans for whom, like the Freikorps [in Germany], the war had not ended. They believed that Vietnam had been lost due to the protesting hippies and corrupt political class who sold out Middle America. The Right had to defeat the enemy at home—the feds and the hippies—to put America to rights, reversing the changes of the civil rights movement and returning the U.S. to its former glory."[10]

Thanks to government overreach by several different uncoordinated, even competing, agencies in pursing Weaver and the botched siege that killed three members of the family all of this playing out on television the image of the right-wing movement took on an aura of victimization by big government. Much public and press questioning ensued. Government investigations determined that the rules of engagement employed in the confrontation were unconstitutional. Weaver's lawsuit against the government was settled in his favor. A sympathetic book and television movie followed, as well a number of ballads, one by the progressive bluegrass musician-composer, Peter Rowan. His "Ruby Ridge" single and the album containing it soared on radio stations' and country and other music charts in 1996, and could be heard played by local musicians unrelated to white nationalism.

Patriot militias sprouted around the country advocating for the citizenry to arm itself and resist federal authorities, accelerating with the federal siege of the Branch Dravidian compound in Waco from February 28, 1993, when the ATF raided and killed five of the members, through April 19, 1993, at which time the compound went up in flames, killing seventy-six people inside, with only nine escaping the fire. One young man, a disgruntled veteran of the 1991 Gulf War, looking for a way to direct his anger at the federal government, was present outside the perimeter of the compound when it burned. Exactly two years later, on April 19, 1995, this man, Timothy McVeigh, parked a truck full of homemade fertilizer explosives in front of the federal building in downtown Oklahoma City. For the Patriot movement, which McVeigh by then identified with, April 19 is a sacred date, the anniversary of the famous 1775 ride of Paul Revere.

The Patriot movement's antigovernment ideology, along with a reverence for private property rights and, of course, the Second Amendment, melded well with the rise of institutionalized libertarianism in the early 1970s, including the founding of the Cato Institute by Charles Koch of the Koch Brothers with their petro-industries fortune and Murray Rothbard, who touted anarchist-capitalism and espoused anti-imperialist and pro-revolutionary views usually identified with the left. Citizens for a Sound Economy was founded in 1984, with Republican U.S. congressman from Texas Ron Paul, a libertarian, as chairman. This organization was the prototype for the later Freedom Works and Americans for Prosperity that spawned the Tea Party demonstrations at the beginning of the Obama administration, in time electing members of Congress and by the end of the Obama presidency, dominating the House of Representatives. In the mix was the rise of Silicon Valley libertarianism, loaded with cash.[11]

The 1970s and 1980s also saw the birth and development of the environmental movement at local, national, and international levels. While often at odds with the mainly white and well-endowed environmental organization, the Native American movement had long fought for their land, water, and treaty rights in the West. In some places, such as Nevada, a coalition of some environmentalists, some ranchers, and the Shoshone and Paiute Indigenous communities took on the federal Bureau of Land Management and other federal agencies controlling the vast public lands in the West that had been taken in wars against the Native peoples in the late nineteenth century and after. At the same time, the "Sagebrush Rebellion," made up of mining, timber, and recreational industries, along with loggers and mill workers, and populated by an array of libertarians, populists, and conservatives, came to be called the "Wise Use" movement, demanding that all federally held lands be turned over to the states and privatized. They had little success until Ronald Reagan was elected in 1980, and appointed one of their number to be Secretary of the Interior, James G. Watt. In addition to fighting to crush the environmental movement, "Wise Use" adherents targeted were the Native American communal holdings under U.S. trust protection, the reservations. A visceral hatred for Mexicans migrating over the southern border was integral to this movement, with its strong white nationalist roots. During the first decade of the new millennium, hard-core white supremacist groups formed militias the "Minutemen" along the Mexican border. Armed anarchists opposed them.[12]

While the "Wise Use" movement, and the later Tea Party movement, presented as grass-roots movements, in reality the driving force and funding came from oil industry megacorporations such as Amoco, British Petroleum, Chevron, and ExxonMobil as well as other giants—Dupont, Yamaha, General Electric, General Motors—and well-endowed organizations including the American Farm Bureau, National Cattlemen's Association, National Rifle Association, Cato Institute, Koch Industries, among many others.[13]

The FBI, during the George W. Bush administration, issued a highly redacted unclassified report titled "White Supremacist Infiltration of Law Enforcement" that warned of a concerted, decades-long attempt by white supremacists to infiltrate police forces. The report states, "The term 'ghost skins' has gained currency among white supremacists to describe those who avoid overt displays of their beliefs to blend into society and covertly advance white supremacist causes."[14] Professor of law and former military police captain Samuel V. Jones, writing about the continual police shootings of young Black men, argued that the incidents should be investigated in light of the FBI report: "Several key events preceded the report. A federal court found that members of a Los Angeles sheriffs department formed a Neo Nazi gang and habitually terrorized the black community. Later, the Chicago police department fired Jon Burge, a detective with reputed ties to the Ku Klux Klan. . . . Thereafter, the Mayor of Cleveland discovered that many of the city police locker rooms were infested with 'White Power' graffiti. Years later, a Texas sheriff department discovered that two of its deputies were recruiters for the Klan." Professor Jones noted that the steep rise in white nationalist groups between 2008 and 2014 grew from 149 to nearly a thousand, which paralleled the rise in police shootings of Black men.[15]

Forty-four percent of military veterans own firearms, and military service is the strongest predictor of gun ownership, according to a survey conducted in 2015.[16] White nationalists also proliferate in all branches of the U.S. military, especially the Army and the Marine Corps. "They call it 'rahowa,'" said T.J. Leyden, "short for racial holy war—and they are preparing for it by joining the ranks of the world's fighting machine, the U.S. military. White supremacists, neo-Nazis and skinhead groups encourage followers to enlist in the Army and Marine Corps to acquire the skills to overthrow what some call the ZOG—the Zionist Occupation Government. Get in, get trained and get out to brace for the coming race war."[17] Leyden served in the Marine Corps from 1988 to 1991 while a member of a white supremacist skinhead group, and has since renounced his former politics. He told Reuters, "I went into the Marine Corps for one specific reason: I would learn how to shoot," so as to take his military skills back to train other proponents of white power.[18] Military authorities make the "few bad apples" argument when queried about the issue, but Leyden claimed that he was very open about his beliefs, including having two-inch Gestapo lighting bolts tattooed about his collar and displaying a Nazi swastika on his locker. The military can also grant what it calls a "moral waiver" to allow felons or other ineligible recruits to join. Such recruits grew from close to 17 percent in 2003 to nearly 20 percent in 2006, according to Pentagon data. Military spokespersons claim that the waiver does not allow racists to join, but their vetting of applicants for white power affiliations is ineffectual. The situation worsened with the endless wars in Iraq and Afghanistan after the new millennium.

For his 2012 book *Irregular Army*, British investigative journalist Matt Kennard carried out extensive interviews with veterans who held extremist views, as well as with leaders of white nationalist groups who encouraged their followers to gain military training for a race war that they planned to provoke. Kennard quotes a 2005 U.S. Department of Defense report: "The Military has a 'don't ask, don't tell" policy pertaining to extremism. If individuals can perform satisfactorily, without making their extremist opinions overt . . . they are likely to be able to complete their contracts."[19]

Although white nationalist groups such as the John Birch Society and White Citizens Councils were founded in the 1950s in response to the Civil Rights movement, the Ku Klux Klan had never lost its white populist support in the South or in industrial urban areas of the North and West. The early Civil Rights movement was strongly committed to nonviolent direct action, which was very effective in garnering widespread exposure in the South, nationally, and internationally. However, in North Carolina, the president of a local Monroe chapter of the NAACP, Robert Williams, who had succeeded in desegregating the local public library and swimming pool in Monroe, called for self-defense against white violence and terrorism. Williams and his partner, Mable Williams, organized the local Black community and formed an armed self-defense group, the Monroe Black Armed Guard. When the couple received death threats and were hit with trumped-up kidnapping charges, they fled to Cuba, where Williams wrote his classic book *Negroes with Guns*.[20] Similarly, in 1964, Black Civil Rights organizers in

Louisiana formed the Deacons of Defense and Justice to provide armed self-defense from the police and the Klan.[21] However, it was not until the 1966 appearance of the Black Panther Party in Oakland, California, that bearing arms emerged as strategic alternative to the nonviolent resistance of the Civil Rights movement.

In response to chronic police violence and abuse in Black communities, Huey Newton conceived of the Black Panthers as a way to monitor police and protect African Americans with armed citizen patrols. California did not restrict the carrying of loaded long guns if the weapon was visible and legally acquired. Very quickly, the California state legislature, backed by the new governor, Ronald Reagan, began working on legislation to outlaw open carry. On May 2, 1967, when the bill was being debated, more than twenty Black Panther women and men, armed with loaded rifles and shotguns, marched up the Capitol lawn and into the Assembly Chamber. They were disarmed and later arrested. At the police station, Bobby Seale read a statement: "The Black Panther party for self-defense calls upon the American people in general and the black people in particular to take careful note of the racist California Legislature which is considering legislation aimed at keeping the black people disarmed and powerless at the very same time that racist police agencies throughout the country are intensifying the terror, brutality, murder and repression of black people."[22] Not only in California, but around the country, states legislated gun regulations.

During the next few years, the Black Panther Party became a national organization with its own newspaper. As local chapters emerged to organize and serve Black communities across the country, federal and state authorities coordinated efforts to target, disrupt, and destroy the organization, and in some cases, engage in assassination, as in the coordinated killing of charismatic Black Panther leader Fred Hampton. The National Rifle Association also became increasingly political during this period. One of the clearest responses to the fears instilled in white people by what came to be termed "urban violence" was the 1972 creation of the National Neighborhood Watch Program, overseen by the National Sheriffs' Association.[23] As Caroline Light observes in *Stand Your Ground: A History of America's Love Affair with Lethal Self-Defense*, "The selective logic of armed citizenship exists interdependently with larger assumptions about criminality. . . . Select law-abiding civilians take on the responsibilities of law enforcement, protecting themselves while policing others…The call for ordinary citizens to serve as quasi-police protectors for their communities assumes that citizens patrolling their neighborhoods are able to differentiate between dangerous criminals and the law-abiding citizens they are tasked to protect, yet the grim reality is that they often make this distinction through the prism of widespread social biases."[24]

This was the case with George Zimmerman, acting on behalf of his Neighborhood Watch program in Sanford, Florida, in February 2012, when he shot and killed Trayvon Martin, a Black teenager who was on his way to his father's home in that very neighborhood. Florida, like many states, had introduced a "stand your ground" law, so the police who came to the scene simply let Zimmerman go after questioning him. Thanks to public outcry, Zimmerman was charged, but he was found not guilty by a jury of six women, all white except for one of mixed Latina heritage.

When Barack Obama was elected president in 2008, white nationalists, many of whom identified as neo-Nazis, along with advocates for "free-market" privatization, geared up to block all social welfare initiatives promised by the Democratic candidate, as well as any policy the Democrats proposed for the following eight years. In 2007, Wall Street housing stocks and mortgage loan institutions had collapsed and unemployment was soaring, mainly among lower-income working-class families. Many of them often people of color could no longer keep up with mortgage payments while unemployed, and lost their homes. Rather than softening the blow with mortgage assistance (bailing out the homeowners), President Obama bailed out the banks and Wall Street. This initial action added fuel to the igniting Tea Party movement. In 2004, the privatization kings David and Charles Koch transformed their lobbying organization into two nonprofits, Americans for Prosperity and FreedomWorks, which became the funding engines and strategy makers for the massive gatherings and demonstrations of righteously angry people drawn into the politics of white nationalism and immigrant (Mexican) hatred. Most important, they also financed electoral campaigns that resulted in the Republican takeover of Congress in 2010.

The election of an African American as president of the United States and commander in chief of its Armed Forces seemed the apocalyptic prophecy of the influential late William Pierce, whose organization National Alliance was one of the most ideologically extreme. Pierce was born in Atlanta; he held a doctorate in physics and was a tenured professor at Oregon State University in 1965, when he became an angry opponent of the Civil Rights movement and the emerging counterculture. He supported George Wallace's presidential campaign and found affinity with neo-Nazi leader George Lincoln Rockwell, who was assassinated in 1967. Pierce then founded his own organization, which became the National Alliance, built with young white men who had supported Wallace. He started a white supremacist publishing house, National Vanguard Books, and put out audio records with hate messages.

Pierce self-published his infamous novel *The Turner Diaries* in 1978, under the pseudonym Andrew Macdonald; it was later reprinted and kept in print by Barricade Books.[25] The book became and remains required reading for white nationalists; Timothy McVeigh had a copy of it in the car he was driving when apprehended by the police soon after the Oklahoma City bombing. The first lines of the novel read, "September 16, 1991. Today it finally began! After all these years of talking—and nothing but talking—we have finally taken our first action. We are at war with the System, and it is no longer a war of words." The story begins when the federal government enforces the "Cohen Act" and raids homes to confiscate all civilian firearms. Turner and his group go underground to overthrow the government, which is controlled by African Americans, with crafty Jews getting them elected and giving them marching orders. This government not only confiscates guns, but also imposes repressive measures under the banner of anti-racism, such as annulling all laws against rape, as these laws are considered racist; making it a hate crime for white people to defend themselves from attacks by people of color; and forcing all citizens to carry passports to move around. Turner witnesses an anti-racist rally in which white people are pulled in and beaten, sometimes killed. The Organization prevails in war, taking regions of the country to operate from, igniting civil war that includes the use of nuclear weapons, by which the Organization destroys New York and Israel. The Soviet Union is destroyed by nuclear war, and then country after country falls apart as anti-Jewish riots destroy their governments. In the novel, people are reading Turner's 1991 diaries in the year 2099: The Organization has conquered the whole world; in Africa, all Black people have been killed; and the continent of Asia has been rendered uninhabitable by radioactive fallout from nuclear bombs. In the United States all people of color were hunted down and killed, and a white nation and white world exists at the end of the twenty-first century.[26]

And it started with the government taking away their guns. So, when young Dylann Roof attempted to start a "race war," he was tapping into the common fear shared by white nationalists, the loss of white supremacy. What was everyday reality during the century of frontier wars from the founding of the United States to the 7th Cavalry massacre at Wounded Knee in 1890, was re-enacted and performed as theater by Roof, but with live ammunition. Liberal and conservative intellectuals and politicians insist that individuals like Roof and the groups they belong to are marginal, but white supremacists are acting and speaking openly in support of the very roots of United States nationalism, embedded in the institutional structure of the country from the Constitution itself, which includes the Second Amendment, to the "lost cause" of the Confederacy to save the institution of slavery and the continued colonization of Native lands. Their words, rhetoric, and desired future differ little from those of the free market fundamentalists and constitutional originalists who actually control the federal institutions and many of the state governments. White nationalists are the irregular forces—the volunteer militias—of the actually existing political-economic order. They are provided for in the Second Amendment.

NINE

ELUDING AND RESISTING THE SECOND AMENDMENT'S HISTORICAL CONNECTION TO WHITE SUPREMACY

In the past, historians have shown little interest in researching the U.S. arms industry, even though gun making was one of the nation's first successful manufacturing industries domestically and globally, and one of the few that escaped deindustrialization. That changed after the U.S. Congress passed the "Protection of Lawful Commerce in Arms Act," effective October 26, 2005, a measure that shields gun manufacturers and licensed dealers from liability for deaths resulting from their products if occurring in a criminal act. With frequent mass shootings in the years before and after, as well as suicides and accidental gun deaths, more scholars and journalists began research into gun violence as a health issue.

Dr. Gerald J. Wintemute, an emergency room physician who has studied gun violence for thirty-five years, experienced research funding drying up. As the director of the Violence Prevention Research Program at the University of

California, Davis Health System, he was virtually alone in the task. But things got worse in 1996, when the Newt Gingrich-led Republican Congress passed the "Dickey Amendment," which barred the Centers for Disease Control and Prevention (CDC) from using federal funds to promote gun regulations, stripping the CDC of the nearly $3 million it had been devoting to the study of injuries and fatalities relating to gun use. While some funds from other federal sources were made available under the Obama administration, the gun-rights debate was highly charged, so that research findings or interpretations could be met with threats of violence. These scholars must take precautions that few in academia find necessary.[1] Even for scholars not researching anything related to guns, there is fear of the 2016 Texas law that extended open-carry rights to public university campuses in the state, leading the president of the faculty senate at the University of Houston to create a PowerPoint presentation to show in faculty forums. One slide suggests that faculty members "may want to be careful discussing sensitive topics; drop certain topics from your curriculum; not 'go there' if you sense anger; limit student access off hours; go to appointment-only office hours; only meet 'that student' in controlled circumstances."[2]

In all the debates and research, little scrutiny is given to the gun manufacturers—the industry itself—with attention mostly directed toward the victims of gun violence, the purchasers and users of firearms, and the gun sellers, particularly those who exhibit at gun shows. The 2016 publication of historian Pamela Haag's meticulously researched and documented book, *The Gunning of America: Business and the*

Making of American Gun Culture[3] was a welcome corrective. The book is a global and detailed survey of the history and present situation of the U.S. firearms industry, containing a more detailed case study of the 150-year history of the Winchester Repeating Arms Company. The founder, Oliver Winchester, had been a shirt maker before he went into the gun business and became a very wealthy Connecticut corporate giant.

In the United States, there is an acute awareness of the powerful influence and grip of corporate advertising, but no other product sold legally on the market bears any similarity to a gun. Guns are made to kill, and except for hunting, that usually means killing other humans or oneself, either intentionally or accidentally. Most critics of easy access to firearms place blame on the N.R.A. for its effective lobbying and for having an outsize influence on its highly active members, suggesting a cult-like relationship. Haag includes the N.R.A. in her condemnation of the unregulated firearms industry, but mainly for the revenue it receives from gun industry advertisements in the organization's publications and on its website. Haag goes to the source and bores in on the gun industry itself as the main culprit, not only ethically, for producing a deadly product, but also for its relentless advertising, which has normalized and domesticated that product, even making getting a gun a coming-of-age milestone for every boy.

Haag writes that her motivation for starting this project was to figure out "what allowed Oliver Winchester and his successors not to feel at least a small bit encumbered by the fact that they manufactured and sold millions of fearfully destructive guns. . . . The gun debate has been mired in rights talk for so long . . . that it is forgotten as a matter of conscience."[4] But what she claims to have discovered in the process is the fallacy of the assumed "gun culture" that historian Richard Hofstadter theorized and which still reigns; rather, she argues, "gun culture" was manufactured by the gun industry and is not some inherent characteristic of U.S. history and society: "An abridged history of the American gun culture, told from legend and popular memory, might go like this: We were born a gun culture. Americans have an exceptional, unique, and timeless relationship to guns, starting with the militias of the Revolutionary War, and it developed on its own from there."[5]

Haag claims that this narrative includes the false assumption that the Second Amendment has always been regarded as a sacred right for the individual to bear arms, and she denies that the idea of gun regulation is new and abnormal. She scoffs at what she calls "the American gun story:"

> The American gun story is about civilians and individual citizens, and they are its heroes or its villains—the frontiersman, the Daniel Boone "long hunter" who trekked far into the wilderness alone, the citizen-patriot militiaman, the guiltily valorized outlaw, and the gun-slinger . . . and this mystique is about individualism: guns protect citizens against overzealous government infringement of liberties; they protect freedom and self-determination.[6]

In making this argument, she dismisses outright any significance of the Second Amendment or of "how the West was won" history: "The story that highlights the Second Amendment, frontiersmen, militias, and the desires and character of the American gun owner is not to be found in the pages of this book."[7]

Haag's work is invaluable for offering a deep study of a particular product and industry; her book resembles those of other contemporary thinkers, such as Mark Kurlansky in *Salt* and *Cod*, and Mark Pendergrast's investigation of the Coca-Cola Corporation. Haag reveals how consumer capitalism works, but she seems not to have a problem with consumer capitalism and advertising per se, only with the fact that the gun has been so culturally normalized that it is sold alongside children's toys, clothing, food, and mouthwash at the low-end chain store such as WalMart, the nation's top seller of guns and ammunition.[8] To support her arguments, not only is the historical context for the Second Amendment ignored, United States history is ignored—absent are the voluntary militias that destroyed Native towns and raped, tortured, and slaughtered the families they found here; no armed slave patrols can be found in her work, no people enslaved, bred, bought, and sold. In accounting for the "celebrity" of the Winchester Model 73, Haag writes: "When considered from a business perspective, however, it becomes clear that the quintessential frontier rifle flourished later, in the 'post-frontier' early 1900s. Its celebrity biography backdated its diffusion and even its popularity." Strangely, the author argues that after the Civil War and a lack of demand for firearms, the Winchester Company suffered a depression in sales, and changed its pitch for selling the rifle from war to "domestic" use:

Winchester's approach meshed with the hard paramilitary realities of conquest and settlement. Indeed, it is worth contemplating how much America's heavily armed civilian population owes to the peculiar domestic nature of both the most cataclysmic nineteenth-century war, the Civil War, and its most violent conquest, of Native American cultures. Unlike in Europe, which kept the U.S. gun business alive, but does not today have our civilian gun violence, in America war and conquest were both domestic, and the guns deployed stayed put within American borders. Western emigrants, de facto, were somewhere between soldier and civilian, their everyday existence to some extent militarized in a land in between battlefield and settlement. In Europe, conquest involved imperial expeditions; America's conquest blurred settler into soldier—and the Model 73, in both design and germinal mystique, suited that hybrid environment.[9]

To the reader, this may sound very much like "gun culture." But, there is a serious problem with Haag's "domestication" of U.S. (and local militia) wars against Native peoples, which were, after all, foreign nations to be conquered, not an inchoate race of random individuals. Referencing only the Indian Wars in the West that followed the Civil War, Haag assumes firearms were not necessary to dispossess and ethnically cleanse the entire eastern half of the continent. In order to make this argument, Haag has to completely ignore the nearly two centuries of Anglo-American colonial violence against Native nations of the Atlantic seaboard, and the aggressive theft of Native land after negotiating international treaties with them as sovereign nations. Nor does she deal with armed slave patrols in the colonies, then in the slave states of the South.

Haag also leaves out the two-year invasion of Mexico and U.S. occupation of Mexico City, with Marines landing in Veracruz and creating a path of destruction filled with corpses of Mexican resisters all the way to the capital, where they ransacked and terrorized the population, while the U.S. Army of the West doubled the country's continental territory by annexing the northern half of Mexico's territory, including the illegally occupied so-called "Texas Republic." It was a two-year foreign war, 1846–48, declared by Congress. It's not clear how Haag comes up with the "domestic" argument, except for the very significant U.S. Civil War, which permanently escalated the level of domestic violence against African-American freedmen. Unfortunately, the discredited ideology of "Manifest Destiny" is the bedrock of Haag's analysis.

The thesis of *The Gunning of America* is that "gun culture" does not exist as a historical and organic reality, but rather as a commercially manufactured ideology created by the gun industry. That can be proven, the author argues, by the fact that there was no gun culture in the nearly two hundred years of the founding and development of the Thirteen British colonies in North America, nor was there such after Independence until the Civil War period in the mid-nineteenth century, when they began to be mass produced and

widely distributed during five years of intense combat. Haag
makes this argument based solely on her assumptions about
technology, the fact that individual gunsmiths made each
firearm, and none were duplicated, plus the fact that ammunition was powder, making the weapon difficult to load and
reload, and clumsy to use. She argues that very few individuals owned guns, that guns were rarely used, and that they
were regarded as simply another tool, like an ax. This argument is made briefly as a backdrop to dismissing the Second
Amendment as meaningful or relevant, maintaining as well
that the militias were ineffective. Then, she plunges into the
study of the rise of the gun industry, mass production, and
the search for markets.

Haag's thesis—particularly her de-emphasis of individual gun ownership, gun culture, and the historical significance of militias in the early Anglo-American colonies and
the early U.S. republic—is identical to the argument made
sixteen years earlier by historian Michael A. Bellesiles in his
discredited book *Arming America: The Origins of a National Gun Culture*. Bellesiles made the same points Haag does
about the paucity of technology before 1850, although Haag
does not "count" guns, or miscount them as Bellesiles did,
or make a clear quantitative argument, which was central
to Bellesiles's project. Haag does not reference Bellesiles's
book or the controversy that followed its publication, but
makes the same argument based on technology, whereas
Bellesiles thesis was based on research into probate records
from the colonial and early national periods that purport-
ed to prove very few households possessed guns. Bellesiles
wrote: "The vast majority of those living in British North

American colonies had no use for firearms, which were cost-ly, difficult to locate and maintain, and expensive to use."[10]

Arming America was released in September 2000—weeks before the Bush v. Gore election and dispute—receiving a long front-page feature review in the *New York Times*, written with glowing eloquence by prestigious University of Chicago historian Garry Wills. That review was followed by an equally uncritical review in the *New York Review of Books* by eminent colonial U.S. historian, Edmund Morgan.[11] This must have been quite heady stuff for an obscure history professor at Emory University in Atlanta, Georgia. A torrent of positive reviews and attention followed in academic publications as well as in the commercial press, including an interview with the author in *Playboy*.

Bellesiles's credibility was enhanced for liberals by the usual pushback and crude membership pile-on from the National Rifle Association, at the time still headed by the obnoxious Charlton Heston, who a few months before the publication of *Arming America* had riveted the audience at the 129th N.R.A. convention, in Charlotte, North Carolina, bellowing, "For the next six months, Al Gore is going to smear you as the enemy. He will slander you as gun-toting, knuckle-dragging, bloodthirsty maniacs who stand in the way of a safer America. Will you remain silent? I will not remain silent. If we are going to stop this, then it is vital to every law-abiding gun owner in America to register to vote and show up at the polls on Election Day." Heston then raised a handmade colonial flintlock long rifle and intoned: "So, as we set out this year to defeat the divisive forces that would take freedom away, I want to say those fighting words for everyone within the sound of my voice to hear and to heed, and especially for you, *Mr. Gore*: 'From my cold, dead hands.'"[12]

In addition to the N.R.A.'s disapproval, there were a few negative reviews of the Bellesiles book by conservative and libertarian magazines such as *National Review* and *Reason*. Yet, within a few months after publication, multiple errors had been identified and discussed online. Meanwhile, in the spring of 2001, the prestigious Bancroft Prize for history went to *Arming America*. It would be a year after the book's publication—in the fall of 2001—that critiques appeared in print in the prestigious peer-reviewed *William and Mary Quarterly*, as well as in law reviews.

A year after questions arose about the book and grew into massive evidence of falsifying sources and misreading others, Northwestern University law professor James Lindgren made an exhaustive study of Bellesiles's arguments and the sources he used to document them, and concluded: "What made the book such a sensation was his description of guns in the seventeenth, eighteenth, and early nineteenth centuries. He claimed that guns were exceptional rather than common, in poor condition even in private hands, not stored in the home but rather in central armories, too expensive to be owned outright by most men, and restricted by law to the Protestant upper and middle classes. None of this is true."[13] Indeed, the opposite was the case—the colonists were armed to the teeth. "Since the book's publication, scholars who have checked the book's claims against its sources have uncovered an almost unprecedented number of discrepancies, errors, and omissions. When these are taken into account, a markedly different picture of colonial America emerges: Household gun ownership in early America was more widespread than today (in a much poorer world)."[14]

The numerous historians and legal specialists who challenged Bellesiles's sparse gun counts found that household gun ownership in comparison to other items owned was high: Bellesiles not only miscounted drastically, he also did no comparative analysis. Lindgren cites a reliable 1774 database of 813 itemized male inventories in which 54 percent of the estates listed guns, compared to only 30 percent of estates listing cash, 14 percent listing swords or edge weapons, 25 percent listing Bibles, 62 percent listing a book other than the Bible, and 79 percent listing any clothes. A search of databases came up with similar numbers, with guns being more common than Bibles and as common as books.

Lindgren writes, "Contrary to *Arming America*'s claims about probate inventories in seventeenth- and eighteenth-century America, there were high numbers of guns, guns were much more common than swords or other edge weapons, women in 1774 owned guns at a rate (18%) higher than Bellesiles claimed men did in 1765–1790 (14.7%), and 83–91% of gun-owning estates listed at least one gun that was not old or broken." Furthermore, "Bellesiles misclassified over 60% of the inventories he examined. He repeatedly counted women as men, counted guns in about a hundred wills that never existed, and claimed that the inventories evaluated more than half of the guns as old or broken when fewer than 10% were so listed." Lindgren found that during period 1765–1790, the 14.7 percent average of estates listing guns that Bellesiles reported is mathematically impossible given the regional averages he reported.[15]

Bellesiles's assessment of the quality and effectiveness of militias was equally misrepresented in his book. One of many instances provided in military historian Robert Churchill's review of the book concerns the Connecticut colony's preparation for war in 1746. Bellesiles wrote that the colony had difficulties in raising troops and finally managed to amass six hundred, but 57 percent were without guns. Churchill looked at the records Bellesiles had cited and found that, on the contrary, of the 454 men mustered, 371 or 81.7 percent had guns, and two of the five units reporting were fully armed, with only one of the five at 57 percent armed. Of the five units reporting their arms, two were 100 percent armed and the worst armed of the other three was 57 percent armed. Professor Lindgren writes about this finding:

> It is hard to know exactly what Bellesiles did, but he may just have seized on the number of the worst-armed unit and reported that number for all units, but only after flipping it to 57% *un*armed. By misleadingly counting the worst-armed unit as the entire company and flipping the results from armed to unarmed, Bellesiles is able to make a very well-armed Connecticut militia (82% armed) appear to be a mostly unarmed militia (43% armed).[16]

Lindgren concludes his exhaustive review of the errors in Bellesiles's account puzzled as to the motives:

The book and the scandal it generated are hard to understand. How could Bellesiles count guns in about a hundred Providence wills that never existed, count guns in San Francisco County inventories that were apparently destroyed in 1906, report national means that are mathematically impossible, change the condition of guns in a way that fits his thesis, misreport the counts of guns in censuses or militia reports, have over a 60% error rate in finding guns in Vermont estates, and have a 100% error rate in finding homicide cases in the Plymouth records he cites? We may never know the truth of why or how *Arming America* made such basic errors, but make them it did.[17]

Bellesiles did not elucidate a political agenda in his densely academic book—and it is unacceptable to admit to a political agenda in the field of academic history. Yet, it does appear that the only explanation as to why he would fabricate and misstate sources was in order to support an unprecedented thesis. Had guns not been widely owned or valued by individuals in colonial Anglo-America, then the Second Amendment to the Constitution could not be interpreted as implying an individual right to bear arms.[18]

Early on, both the American Historical Association and the Organization of American Historians officially defended Bellesiles's scholarship and objected to the right-wing attacks, and those of gun advocates, on his book. And even after the publication of Lindgren's compilation of errors in the book, some historians continued to promote and affirm its thesis while admitting that some errors had been made.

One such prominent historian was Jon Wiener, a prolific author and professor of History at the University of California, Irvine. In an article for *The Nation*, Wiener related that when Bellesiles appeared at the Irvine campus to talk about the controversy in early 2001, there were "unusually large men," one wearing a flak jacket and another with a shaved head, distributing a brochure titled "The Lies of Michael Bellesiles."

> The large men were activists in the pro-gun, anti-Bellesiles movement, which had been campaigning to discredit his work since before the publication of *Arming America* by Knopf in September 2000. The book argues that our picture of guns in early America is all wrong: the picture where America is settled by men with guns, hunting game and fighting Indians; where, in 1776, militiamen grabbed their guns to go fight for independence; where the Founding Fathers protected individuals' right to own guns. Bellesiles argues that instead, gun culture is a fairly recent development in American history. . . . Not until the Civil War put guns in the hands of millions of men did gun culture flourish.[19]

Wiener pointed out in the article that there were clear "political implications" in the thesis that threatened the National Rifle Association.

The Second Amendment, this suggests, was not adopted to protect the widespread ownership or popularity of guns—it was instead intended to address the inadequacy of the weapons in the hands of local militias, on which the early nation relied in the absence of a standing army. So gun-rights groups targeted Bellesiles and his book, and large men in flak jackets came to his talk at Irvine and other places.[20]

In light of the questions being raised, Bellesiles's employer, Emory University, launched an internal and external inquiry that found Bellesiles's scholarship unsatisfactory, which Bellesiles challenged, but then he suddenly resigned in late October 2002. In December 2002, Columbia University, which awards the Bancroft Prize, rescinded the award that had gone to *Arming America*, stating that the author had "violated basic norms of scholarship and the high standards expected of Bancroft Prize winners."[21] Moreover, the publisher, Knopf, did not renew Bellesiles's contract for the book and ceased publication. In 2003, a small, independent publisher in San Francisco, Soft Skull Press, gained rights to the book and issued a new edition that remains in print. Historians Gary Wills and Edmund Morgan expressed regret that they had been taken in by the book and moved on, as did most historians, assuming the matter was resolved.

However, historian Jon Wiener never budged in his support for Bellesiles. In his 2005 book *Historians in Trouble: Plagiarism, Fraud, and Politics in the Ivory Tower*, Wiener places Bellesiles in the category of "Those Who Were Burned," writing that after receiving high praise and an award for his book on guns, the gun lobby destroyed Bellesiles's career, with the scholars who challenged the work apparently sheepishly complying, since "the critics came up with no evidence of intentional deception, no evidence of invented documents." Wiener's thesis is that some historians are punished or discredited while others are hardly touched by controversy, such as in the case of plagiarism by the renowned academics Doris Kearns Goodwin and Stephen Ambrose, which he attributes to the relative power of the historian involved, but especially to the power of groups outside the history profession.[22]

In 2010, the New Press, which had published Wiener's book five years earlier, released a new book by Michael Bellesiles, *1877: America's Year of Living Violently*. The galleys sent to reviewers noted:

> A major new work of popular history, *1877* is also notable as the comeback book for a celebrated U.S. historian. Michael Bellesiles is perhaps most famous as the target of an infamous "swiftboating" campaign by the National Rifle Association, following the publication of his Bancroft Prize–winning book *Arming America* (Knopf, 2000)—"the best kind of non-fiction," according to the *Chicago Tribune*—which made daring claims about gun ownership in early America. In what became the history profession's most talked-about and notorious case of the past generation, *Arming America* was eventually discredited after an unprecedented and controversial review called into question its sources, charges

which Bellesiles and his many prominent supporters have always rejected.[23]

Scott McLemee, the "Intellectual Affairs" columnist
for *Inside Higher Ed*, was appalled at this deceptive advance
publicity, especially the mention of the Bancroft Prize without clarifying that it had been rescinded:

> Bellesiles has a certain claim to fame, certainly, but
> not as "the target of an infamous 'swiftboating'
> campaign."[24] He is, and will be forever remembered
> as, a historian whose colleagues found him to have
> violated his profession's standards of scholarly in-
> tegrity. . . . It is true that he drew the ire of the Na-
> tional Rifle Association, and I have no inclination
> to give that organization's well-funded demagogy
> the benefit of any doubt. But gun nuts did not force
> Bellesiles to do sloppy research or to falsify sources.
> That his scholarship was grossly incompetent on
> many points is not a "controversial" notion. Nor is
> it open to dispute whether or not he falsified sourc-
> es. That has been exhaustively documented by his
> peers. To pretend otherwise is itself demagogic.
>
> If a major commercial press wants to help a
> disgraced figure make his comeback, that is one
> thing, but rewriting history is another.[25]

Many of the comments following McLemee's article,
however, defended Bellesiles's thesis, while the majority of
others thought he should at least be given a second chance.

Meanwhile, as cited earlier, most liberal journalists and historians continue to make similar arguments that dismiss the Second Amendment, without citing the Bellesiles book or the controversy, as Haag does in *The Gunning of America*. However, it really *is* possible to discredit the Second Amendment without rewriting U.S. history; in fact, it is possible by writing accurate U.S. history. For those who see the Second Amendment as permission to own personal firearms without regulations and to carry them in public places, as well as those who insist that the Second Amendment doesn't mean what it says and revise history to fit the argument, it seems the histories of racial domination, land theft, and genocide from which the Second Amendment emerged are impossible to confront, or that sublimated history is acted out in deranged ways, such as through mass shootings, police killings of unarmed Black people, or as Sarah Winchester did, defending oneself from the ghosts of slaughtered Indians.

Fifty miles south of San Francisco is a Victorian home billed as a "ghost house" on billboards that start appearing in Oregon to the north and San Diego to the south. Winchester Rifle heiress Sarah L. Winchester, the wealthy widow of William Wirt Winchester, bought the house in the late 1880s and soon began building additions. By the time of her death nearly forty years later, the home covered six acres, containing hundreds of rooms, including ten thousand windows, forty-seven fireplaces, thirteen bathrooms, and six kitchens. Some of the forty stairways and two thousand doors lead nowhere.[26] Tradesmen and craftsmen worked dawn to dusk daily and were still at work the day of her death. The tourist literature and published accounts, as well as the Hollywood movie about Sarah Winchester,[27] portray her as a deranged crazy lady, a character in a ghost story, yet for nearly three decades, she personally designed every detail and worked directly with the builders.

Her stated purpose? To elude ghosts.

In 1885, Sarah Winchester moved to northern California from the family home in Connecticut, a seven-day train journey. The railroad for two decades had transported and continued to transport the guns and cartridges manufactured by the family business along the same route. As it did, Winchesters were in the hands of the Army posted to fend off Indigenous residents opposed to the intrusion of the rails in their territories. The weapons were also used to kill off the buffalo, the Native food supply, until, by the time of Sarah's journey, there were only a few hundred left out of the 30 million that existed two decades earlier.

When settlers, railroad workers, and soldiers thought of a gun, they conjured a rifle, and its name was Winchester, generic, just as the brand name Kleenex is generic for facial tissue of any brand. On passenger trains at the time, hired staff told triumphant stories about killing Indians and buffalo. The railroad narratives were printed and survive, one example telling of an Army major's heroics: "As an Indian fighter he had no superior. . . . He cleaned out whole tribes of hostiles." Another told of one stop on the route, Fort Kearny, where Buffalo Bill had killed his first Indian with his trusted Winchester, and took the scalp as a souvenir. Passengers were also loaned Winchesters to shoot buffalo out of the train widows as they traveled across the Plains.

By the mid-1880s, as Mrs. Winchester traveled through

the territory, adult Indigenous refugees of genocidal war had been disarmed, half starved, and held in concentration camps, their children taken to far-away residential schools, when they created a form of resistance that spread like wildfire in all directions from its source. A Paiute holy man, Wovoka, in Nevada. Indigenous pilgrims, including the Lakota holy man Sitting Bull, clandestinely journeyed to Nevada to receive instructions on how to perform the Ghost Dance, which promised to make the invaders disappear and the buffalo return, allowing those loved ones killed by bullets to return as well. It was a simple dance performed by everyone, requiring only a specific kind of shirt made of feed sack and hung with colored ribbons that was to protect the dancers from gunfire.

When the dancing began in December 1890 among the Lakota at the Pine Ridge Army Control Center, officials reported it as disturbing and unstoppable, warning Washington of a possible armed uprising. Sitting Bull was assumed to be the instigator of the dancing, so they put him under house arrest, heavily guarded. Sitting Bull was assassinated by one of his guards on December 15, 1890. But the dancing continued, culminating in the U.S. Army's slaughter of three hundred unarmed and starving Lakota refugees attempting to turn themselves in to the Army. Blood-soaked Lakota survivors were dragged into a nearby church. It being Christmastime, the sanctuary was candlelit and decked with greenery. In the front, a banner read: PEACE ON EARTH AND GOOD WILL TO MEN. The dancing stopped.

In official U.S. military annals, the massacre is called a victorious battle. Congressional Medals of Honor were bestowed on twenty of the soldiers involved in the killing.

L. Frank Baum, a Dakota Territory settler later famous for writing *The Wonderful Wizard of Oz*, edited the *Aberdeen Saturday Pioneer* at the time. He wrote, "Our only safety depends upon the total extermination of the Indians. Having wronged them for centuries we had better, in order to protect our civilization, follow it up by one more wrong and wipe these untamed and untamable creatures from the face of the earth."

And so it makes sense that Mrs. Winchester felt the need to guard herself from the ghosts of those killed by the Winchester repeating rifle

Visitors trekking through the widow's home are amused, then saddened, by the evidence all around them of the fears and anguish of a mentally disturbed person. The tour guides and literature point to the case of a seriously deluded rich woman. Yet there is another possibility, a message, a warning: that the house is a kind of hologram in the minds of each and every person on the continent, just barely below their consciousness.

Pamela Haag's history of the Winchester Repeating Arms Company gives credit to the agency of Sarah Winchester. But the author attributes Sarah's obsession with ghosts to the general popularity of "spiritualism" in the late nineteenth century, and deems Sarah highly efficient and functional despite her obsession with ghosts. The U.S. savage war against the Lakota and Cheyenne that was taking place at the time does not appear in Haag's account of Sarah Winchester's fears. Haag does not even mention the Ghost Dance and the Wounded Knee massacre, which had to have affected Sarah Winchester profoundly.[28]

Any assessment of gun violence and the Second Amendment in the United States is incomplete or skewed without dealing with what the guns were for, and, given what they were for, what that means about their popularity and proliferation today. The United States created its armed forces and police to carry out a genocidal policy against Native peoples, seize Native land, and control African Americans, which continues to this day in other forms, including police shooting unarmed Black men and incarcerating a large percentage of them. In the process, the United States has invented enemies and spent hoards of wealth to erect the largest military force in history, including a vast network of hundreds of military bases in more than seventy countries and territories around the globe. In some regards, the official narratives the nation has formed to dissociate the Second Amendment from the atrocities it was used to commit are like the extensions on Sarah Winchester's house, constructed so that The People can more comfortably elude the fellow human beings whose lives and land have been stolen, and whose names, traditions, and memories we are well armed to forget.

HISTORY IS NOT PAST

On June 22, 2016, following the horrific slaughter in Orlando ten days earlier that took forty-nine lives, a small group of Congressional Democrats staged an unprecedented live-streamed, twenty-five-hour sit-in led by former Civil Rights icon Congressman John Lewis. The protest grew to 170 lawmakers sitting on the floor of the House of Representatives singing "We Shall Overcome" and demanding a gun-control bill.[1]

Earlier in the week, the Republican-controlled Senate had rejected several gun-control proposals, one of which would have prohibited gun sales to all those listed on the Terrorist Screening Center's "no-fly" list of suspected terrorists.[2] Democrats had seized the Orlando tragedy as an opportunity to raise the ban, because the FBI had investigated Omar Mateen, the Orlando shooter, for possible terrorist leanings, but had not placed his name on the no-fly list. Even some supporters of gun control who were also concerned about the burgeoning security state were troubled by demands to expand the demonstrably flawed no-fly list.[3]

No legislation resulted from the action. Maine

Republican Senator Susan Collins drew up a compromise bipartisan proposal, supported by prominent Democrats, but it was not scheduled for a vote. The gun-control lawmakers blamed N.R.A. pressure on their Republican counterparts. Albeit without success in passing legislation, the sit-in received positive mainstream press coverage and public approval. Polls had long shown support for restrictions on gun sales and use, as well as support for background checks at gun shows. By 2016, nearly two-thirds of those polled favored stricter laws, and majorities even supported nationwide bans on the sale of semiautomatic weapons such as the AR-15, and on the sale of magazines holding more than ten bullets. A majority also preferred that across-the-board federal laws should be created, rather than continuing the patchwork state regulations or lack thereof. Super-majorities of both Democrats and Republicans who were polled supported background checks at gun shows and in private sales. Even Justice Scalia in the Supreme Court's *Heller* opinion, which found the Second Amendment to be an individual constitutional right, made clear that the decision did not bar gun regulation.[4]

While the sit-in was taking place, London's *Daily Guardian* brought attention to a report released by the prestigious *Journal of the American Medical Association*: "Following enactment of gun law reforms in Australia in 1996, there were no mass firearm killings through May 2016. There was a more rapid decline in firearm deaths between 1997 and 2013 compared with before 1997 but also a decline in total non-firearm suicide and homicide deaths of a greater magnitude."[5]

The Australian gun-control regulations and gun buy-back took place soon after the April 28–29, 1996, mass shooting in a favorite Australian tourist spot, Port Arthur, on the Australian island of Tasmania, which had its own haunted history: Between 1825 and 1832, British settlers in Australia carried out a genocidal campaign that nearly wiped out the Indigenous Tasmanians, and during the rest of the century, hunted and killed the survivors for sport. In the 1966 mass shooting, thirty-five Euro-Australians were left dead and twenty-three wounded. Marin Bryant, the shooter, was a twenty-eight-year-old Euro-Australian who survived, was tried, and although deemed mentally impaired, was found guilty and received a life sentence for each fatality, without possibility of parole, as Australia, like European and Latin American countries, does not have the death penalty.

The Australian people were in a state of shock following the massacre. In proportion to its population, Australia had experienced its share of mass shootings in the previous two decades. The country was among the top ten purchasers of personal firearms, as it had no domestic manufacturers. Prime Minister John Howard quickly put forward a strict gun-control package that became the National Firearms Programme Implementation Act of 1996, which passed with the support of all political parties as well as local governments.

The Australian gun-control success story was seized on as a model by gun-control advocates in the United States, particularly following the 1999 Columbine High School mass shooting. Yet, despite many similarities between the racial violence and genocide that accompanied Europeans settling on Indigenous land in Australia and the United States, and the emergence of similar gun cultures in both countries, the Australian example has yet to prove an effective tool for enacting legislation in the U.S. Congress. The main difference between Australia and the United States is the Second Amendment. Neither Australia, nor any other country, has any such a constitutional or legal measure.

Certainly the National Rifle Association carries weight through the persistent agitation of some of its most dedicated members, but they can hardly be the cause of the apparent lack of enthusiasm and depth to gun-control efforts, making it impossible to even refer to a gun-control "movement." Except in African American communities, particularly in Chicago, there has been little passion for gun control woven into the fabric of the culture at the local level, so that those who support gun control appear to be isolated individuals or small civic groups without membership representation, while the majority of the population passively supports gun regulations. Three days after the mass shooting in Las Vegas, Hahrie Han, a professor of political science at the University of California, Santa Barbara specializing in U.S. civic associations and leadership, contributed an op-ed piece to the New York Times contending that an activist-based organizaorganization such as the N.R.A. can only be challenged by an equally activist-based organization for effective gun control, arguing that money, petitions, and classic lobbying will not work:

> Understanding the choices gun-control advocates have begins with understanding where the outsize power of the National Rifle Association originates.

... Most people assume its power comes from money. The truth is that gun-control advocates have lots of money, too. Billionaires like Michael Bloomberg have pledged fortunes to supporting gun control. ... The N.R.A.'s power is not just about its money or number of supporters or a favorable political map. It has also built something that gun-control advocates lack: an organized base of grass-roots power. .... Local gun clubs and gun shops provide a similar structure for the gun-rights movement. There are more gun clubs and gun shops in the United States than there are McDonald's.[6]

This situation must be due in large measure to the fact that the great majority of U.S. citizens accept the Second Amendment as an individual constitutional right and view the Constitution as sacred. Following the 2008 Heller decision, Gallup asked in a poll: "Do you believe the Second Amendment to the U.S. Constitution guarantees the rights of Americans to own guns, or do you believe it only guarantees members of state militias such as the National Guard units the right to own guns?" Seventy-three percent agreed it was an individual right, while 20 percent said it was not.[7]

Perhaps reverence for the Second Amendment and the privileging of individual rights over collective rights, not the N.R.A., are the source of the problem with enacting firearms regulations. Some even argue convincingly that the N.R.A. is losing members among the majority of sportsmen, who feel they are getting a bad name due to the N.R.A.'s alignment with the political right.[8]

Mark Ames's 2005 book *Going Postal: Rage, Murder, and Rebellion: From Reagan's Workplaces to Clinton's Columbine and Beyond*,[9] tended to blame mass shootings on inchoate gun craziness, and, as he put it a few days after the Sandy Hook mass killings, "the hick fascism of the NRA."[10] Three years later, in the wake of the Charleston church massacre, he wrote:

> But it's not enough to call them irrational, un-normal, or gun-nuts—the real question is why, from a Darwinism-of-politics standpoint, the gun-nut cult has proved to be so successful. What is it about the gun cultists' fanaticism and paranoia that has made them thrive as a force in the post–New Deal ecosystem, as opposed to so many other sects here fueled by fanaticism, paranoia, and petty malice?[11]

Ames focuses on the promotion of individualism by the ruling class of corporate giants to explain why the gun situation is allowed to exist in a modern industrial society, arguing that gun-rights politics fit with the corporate agenda that profits from atomized individualism. "If all you do when you think of guns is think of an instrument that is dangerous, can kill, and is usually seen being waved around by dangerous criminals or pot-bellied white jerks in pickups, then you don't see the angles." He rightly dismisses the idea that the wealthy fear an armed populace; rather, what they worry about is government regulations on their capacity to make profit, and this is increasingly the case with the tech industry. Ames asks: "So why does the Big Business lobby align so seamlessly with the gun cultists?" He recognizes that Second Amendment advocates, nearly 75 percent of the population, truly believe that guns are a source of political rights and political power: "That guns in fact are the *only* source of political power. . . . If you think guns, rather than concentrated wealth, equals political power, then you'd resent government power far more than you'd resent billionaires' power or corporations' hyper-concentrated wealth/power, because government will always have more and bigger guns. In fact you'd see pro-gun, anti-government billionaires like the Kochs as your natural political allies in your gun-centric notion of political struggle against the concentrated gun power of government."[12]

Ames's argument reflects contemporary reality, but it also extends from a much deeper historical dance between the wealthy and politically powerful, who dominate the economic and social order by making sure some symbolic power sedates those who actually have little financial leverage and thus, extremely limited political power.

It is the case that for rural settlers of the North American British colonies, and for U.S. American settlers after Independence, a firearm was regarded as a necessary utensil for the settler's task—as with a hoe, an ax, a team of oxen or horses—a point made by some gun-control advocates as evidence that guns were meaningless. However, it's illogical to assume that the gun's utilitarian role outweighed the immediate sense of power and domination that firearms offer. The land that the hoe, the ax, the ox, and the slave's body were used to cultivate was taken by armed force and repression; the land was already home to Indigenous societies that for millennia had been engaged in agricultural and animal husbandry, and had developed distinct languages, cultures, and traditions. That is the way of settler-colonialism, and that is the way of the gun—to kill off enemies and, in the case of the North American colonies and the independent United States, to control African Americans. Violence perpetrated by armed settlers, even genocide, were not absent in the other territories where the British erected settler-colonies—Australia, Canada, and New Zealand but the people of those polities never declared the gun a God-given right; only the founding fathers of the United States did that. And the people of the other Anglo settler-colonies did not have economies, governments, and social orders based on the enslavement of other human beings. The United States is indeed "exceptional," just not in the way usually intoned by politicians and patriots.

Wyoming Senator Alan Simpson put it succinctly: "Without guns, there would be no West," adding that his grandfather had settled in the Wyoming territory two years before Custer's defeat by the Sioux and the Cheyenne nations at the Little Big Horn.[13] "The West," of course, is a metaphor for the continent, as it began on the Atlantic seaboard. But in this interview Simpson was not only speaking historically about what the guns were for—to kill Indians, always the implied enemy, in order to seize more land—he was promoting gun rights in the present. He pointed out in another interview that in Wyoming, "how steady you hold your rifle, that's gun control in Wyoming."[14] Here Simpson reveals that when firearms were no longer needed to appropriate Indigenous Peoples' lands, the firearm became a representation of ongoing racist domination—a kind of war trophy—not just of Native Peoples and their territories, but of African Americans and the world. The degree of racist pathology inherent in this perspective has become so normalized that it was barely news when George Zimmerman openly auctioned the gun he used to kill Trayvon Martin, selling it for $250,000 to a mother who bought the gun as a birthday present for her son.[15] In his auction listing "Mr. Zimmerman touted the weapon, a Kel-Tec PF-9, as 'an American firearm icon'"[16] and vowed to help stop the Black Lives Matter movement. "Regeneration through violence," is what Richard Slotkin calls the martial tradition that goes to the root of the founding and behavior of the U.S. settler-state in the world after the "closing of the frontier," which continues to this day domestically in multiple violent forms.[17]

The elephant in the room in these debates has long been what the armed militias of the Second Amendment were to be used for. The kind of militias and gun rights of the Second Amendment had long existed in the colonies and were expected to continue fulfilling two primary roles in the United States: destroying Native communities in the armed march to possess the continent, and brutally subjugating the enslaved African population that is, the control of land and people, and using them disposably for profit. But this is not just history.

The renewed gun culture and the transformation of the N.R.A. coincided with the end of the Vietnam War. Vietnam was not the first twentieth-century "Indian war," meaning U.S. military interventions attacking noncombatants, burning their homes and fields, and conducting operations to search, destroy, and kill anything that moves.[18] The United States invaded the Philippines in 1898 and occupied the country for the following forty-eight years.[19] Under the pretense of supporting a force of thirty thousand indigenous Filipino rebels who had just fought and won independence from Spain, the United States brought in two hundred thousand of its troops to carry out a three-year search-and-destroy war that left 20 percent of the Filipino population dead, mostly civilians.[20] A U.S. commander, Admiral Dewey, referred to the Filipinos as "the Indians" and vowed to "enter the city [Manila] and keep the Indians out." Twenty-six of the thirty U.S. generals in the Philippines had been officers in the North American "Indian wars."[21] When Theodore Roosevelt became president and oversaw the war, he referred to the Filipino independence leader Aguinaldo as a "renegade Pawnee" and observed that Filipinos did not have the right to govern their country just because they happened to occupy it.[22]

Other twentieth-century U.S. military operations were carried out in Haiti and Nicaragua, the latter a prolonged counterinsurgency against a guerrilla resistance led by Augusto Sandino to drive out the occupying U.S. Marines and the U.S. Standard Fruit Company (now the Dole Food Company) and other corporations stripping the northeastern Nicaraguan tropical rain forest of its resources and ecology. The Marines left, but not until they had trained a vicious national guard under the first Somoza who then had Sandino assassinated.[23]

The Vietnam War was something different, going from small units to all-out invasion, a half million U.S. servicemen on the ground, yet it too became a brutal savage war that targeted civilians. Following the 1954 defeat and withdrawal of French occupation forces, the Eisenhower administration, already aiding the French efforts to prevent Vietnam's independence, took over the counterinsurgency; this morphed into full military invasion and occupation of the South of the country in 1965, continuing another decade until the United States was also defeated and fled.

The narratives of the U.S. anti-war movement's success often give the impression that there was widespread dissent against the Vietnam War, but this was not the case until the late 1960s, with bitter divisions, the majority of both the elite and the organized labor movement (still mostly white and male) strongly favoring the war; the majority who then turned against the war believed it could not be won. The burgeoning right-wing movement made significant gains during the war, with anticommunism a major bludgeon. With the humiliating U.S. military defeat and the war-induced economic depression that followed as well as intense government repression against the Civil Rights movement, which had gone national during the 1960s the right wing had by the late 1970s built an infrastructure of media, think tanks, and organized electoral constituencies that have been increasingly dominant ever since. No apologies or reparations have been offered by any subsequent administration, and the war, even at its fiftieth anniversary, was officially deemed a failed effort but a "noble cause" by the Obama administration.[24] Even the date that the U.S. government uses as the historical start of its war against Vietnam, March 1965, ignores the fact that U.S. military operations there began a decade earlier.[25] Perhaps the event that will shape the future narrative of the war is Ken Burns's 18-hour patriotic documentary *The Vietnam War*, which premiered on PBS in September 2017.[26]

The populist frontier ideology has served the U.S. ruling class well for its entire history and once again found tremendous resonance in the Vietnam War as another Indian war. A key to John F. Kennedy's political success was that he revived the "frontier" as a trope of populist imperialism, speaking of the "settling" of the continent and "taming" a different sort of "wilderness." In Kennedy's acceptance speech in Los Angeles at the 1960 Democratic Convention, he said: "I stand tonight facing west on what was once the last frontier. From the lands that stretch 3,000 miles behind me, the pioneers of old gave up their safety, their comfort and sometimes their lives to build a new world here in the West. . . . We stand today on the edge of a new frontier." The metaphor described Kennedy's plan for employing political power to make the world the new frontier of the United States. Central to this vision was the Cold War, what Richard Slotkin calls "a *heroic* engagement in the 'long twilight struggle' against communism," to which the nation was summoned by Kennedy in his inaugural address. Soon after he took office, that struggle took the form of the counterinsurgency program in Vietnam and his creation of the Green Beret Special Forces. "Seven years after Kennedy's nomination," Slotkin reminds us, "American troops would be describing Vietnam as 'Indian Country' and search-and-destroy missions as a game of 'Cowboys and Indians'; and Kennedy's ambassador to Vietnam would justify a massive military escalation by citing the necessity of moving the 'Indians' away from the 'fort' so that the 'settlers' could plant 'corn.'"[27]

On January 2, 2016, armed men arrived at the Malheur National Wildlife Refuge in Oregon and began an occupation of the headquarters and surrounding territory for the next forty days.[28] In 1908, President Theodore Roosevelt had carved out and appropriated most of Northern Paiute territory in Oregon, territory guaranteed by treaty; this then became the Malheur National Wildlife Refuge in Oregon. It was a part of Roosevelt's "wilderness" conservation project that annexed dozens of Indigenous sacred sites, such as Yellowstone, Yosemite, and Grand Canyon, calling the federal theft "national parks." Most Native land in the West was seized without the agreement of Native nations as "public domain," and ever since has been leased at minimal cost to corporations and individuals for private ranching, and to corporations for commercial mining, oil drilling and pipelines, and timber cutting. The private exploitation of public lands is in addition to the vast privately owned ranch lands grabbed by settler-ranchers under federal homesteading measures in the wake of the ethnic cleansing of Native communities by the U.S. Army of the West.[29]

Wealthy cattle ranchers like those who seized Malheur have long been lobbying and clamoring for the federal public lands to be transferred to the states, which, unlike the federal government, can sell off land and privatize all of it. In light of Native peoples' demands for restitution of sacred sites and all federal- and state-held lands that were taken without treaties or agreements, this is a continuation of the

Indian wars, fronted by ranching and fossil-fuel resource interests, but made possible by the continuing U.S. system of colonialism and a public blinded to its history. All these sacred sites and "public" lands must be returned to the stewardship of the Native nations from which they were illegally seized; none should be privatized. Malheur was indeed a "skirmish among colonizers."[30]

Rapper Ice-T, in an interview in London soon after the Aurora, Colorado, movie house slaughter, was asked his opinion of guns in the U.S. and the gun-control effort. He replied "Well, that's not going to change anything in the United States, no. United States is based on guns. Like KRS says, you'll never have justice on stolen land."[31]

ACKNOWLEDGMENTS

I'm honored to be among the estimable authors who have published timely books in the Open Media Series of City Lights Publishers. I thank the founder and editor of the Open Media Series, Greg Ruggiero, for seeing potential for a different kind of book on the much debated Second Amendment. Thanks also to the wonderful City Lights Publishing and Marketing Director Stacey Lewis, and City Lights Publisher Elaine Katzenberger. I'm forever grateful to Lawrence Ferlinghetti for founding City Lights Bookstore and Publishing and keeping it going for more than six decades, thriving now more than ever.

This book would not have been possible without the rich literature on the Second Amendment, mass shootings, gun rights, and gun control that has been produced already in the 21st century. Although my interpretation of the history of the Second Amendment and the distinctive U.S. American culture that finds itself unique among countries in private gun ownership with minimal laws controlling ownership and use, differs considerably from previous works, I appreciate the dedicated research and writing that has gone into the many books and articles that I cite in this text.

Some of the historical material and interpretations in *Loaded* are drawn from my book *An Indigenous Peoples' History of the United States*, published by Beacon Press in 2014. I want to acknowledge my remarkable editors there, Gayatri Patnaik and Rachael Marks.

I also want to thank Johanna Fernández for her close reading and suggestions, as well as Steve Hiatt, who read an early draft chapter on Missouri Confederate guerrillas, offering supportive comments and encouragement.

Finally, I wish to thank many friends and relatives who tolerated my incessant talk about guns in United States history these past two years.

NOTES

INTRODUCTION

1. "Firearms Numbers in the United States 1945–2012," *Gun Watch*, June 28, 2015. Accessed July 29, 2017: http://gunwatch.blogspot.com/2015/06/firearms-numbers-in-united-states-1945.html

2. Evan Osnos, "Making a Killing: The business and politics of selling guns," *The New Yorker*, June 27, 2016. The kinds of weapons include 110 million handguns and the same number of rifles, plus 86 million shotguns.

3. Richard Hofstadter, *Harper's Magazine*, November 1964. Accessed July 31, 2017: https://harpers.org/archive/1964/11/the-paranoid-style-in-american-politics/

4. Ibid.

5. Senator Barack Obama, while campaigning for the presidency in 2008, was recorded saying to a private donors' gathering in San Francisco that disaffected white people "cling to their guns and religion." Ed Pilkington, "Obama Angers Midwest Voters with Guns and Religion Remark, *The Guardian*, April 14, 2008.

6. Warren E. Burger, "The Right to Bear Arms," *Parade*, January 14, 1990, p. 4.

7. "Open Carry," Law Center to Prevent Gun Violence. Accessed July 29, 2017: http://smartgunlaws.org/gun-laws/policy-areas/firearms-in-public-places/open-carrying/

8. Jiaquan Xu, M.D.; Sherry L. Murphy, B.S.; Kenneth D. Kochanek, M.A.; and Brigham A. Bastian, "Deaths: Final Data for 2013, *National Vital Statistics Reports*, Vol. 64, No. 2; p. 84, table 18. Accessed June 19, 2017: www.cdc.gov/nchs/data/nvsr/nvsr64/nvsr64_02.pdf

9. Sharon LaFraniere, Sarah Cohen and Richard A. Oppel Jr., "How Often Do Mass Shootings Occur? On Average, Every Day, Records Show," *New York Times*, December 2, 2015. Accessed June 13, 2017: www.nytimes.com/2015/12/03/us/how-often-do-mass-shootings-occur-on-average-every-day-records-show.html?smid=tw-share

10. Eyder Peralta, "Study: Most Gun Deaths Happen Outside of Mass Shootings," *the two-way*, National Public Radio, February 1, 2013. Accessed June 19, 2017: www.npr.org/sections/

thetwo-way/2013/02/01/170872321/study-most-gun-deaths-happen-outside-of-mass-shootings

11. Nate Silver, "Did Democrats Give Up in the Gun Control Debate?" *New York Times*, January 11, 2011.

12. David Cole, "The Terror of Our Guns," *New York Review of Books*, July 14, 2016.

13. Ibid., referring to the claim made in one of the books reviewed by Cole on the history of the gun industry, with the Winchester Rifle Company the central case study: Pamela Haag, *The Gunning of America: Business and the Making of American Gun Culture*, New York: Basic Books, 2916. The other two books Cole reviews are: Robert J. Spitzer, *Guns Across America: Reconciling Gun Rules and Rights*, New York: Oxford University Press, 2015; and Firmin DeBrabander, *Do Guns Make Us Free? Democracy and the Armed Society*, New Haven: Yale University Press, 2015. Spitzer argues that the regulation of guns from the time they were invented, including throughout U.S. history, is not a contradiction to the Second Amendment or to the Heller decision as individual rights. See also: Mark Anthony Frassetto, *Firearms and Weapons Legislation up to the Early 20th Century*. Washington, DC: Georgetown University Law Center, 2013). This history ends in 1935, but many of the laws are still in effect.

14. Michael Waldman, *The Second Amendment: A Biography*. New York: Simon and Schuster, 2015. Waldman is president of the Brennan Center for Justice at NYU School of Law, a nonpartisan law and policy institute. See also on the Second Amendment: William Briggs, *How America Got Its Guns: A History of the Gun Violence Crisis*. Albuquerque: University of New Mexico Press, 2017, pp. 75–108.

15. *The Congress shall have Power To provide for organizing, arming, and disciplining, the Militia, and for governing such Part of them as may be employed in the Service of the United States, reserving to the States respectively, the Appointment of the Officers, and the Authority of training the Militia according to the discipline prescribed by Congress. . . .*

16. Nancy Isenberg, *White Trash: The 400-Year Untold History of Class in America*. New York: Viking, 2016, pp. 7–39.

17. Charles Sellers, *The Market Revolution: Jacksonian America, 1815–1846*. New York: Oxford University Press, 1994, p. 9.

CHAPTER ONE

1. For the central role of George Washington as a land speculator and colonial militia leader in the French and Indian War, see: William Hogeland, *Autumn of the Black Snake: The Creation of the U.S. Army and*

the Invasion That Opened the West, New York: Farrar, Straus and Giroux, 2017, pp. 3–80.

2. John Grenier, *The First Way of War: American War Making on the Frontier, 1607–1814*. New York: Cambridge University Press, 2005, p. 147.

3. Joseph Doddridge, *Notes on the Settlement and Indian Wars of the Western Parts of Virginia and Pennsylvania from 1763 to 1783, Inclusive, Together with a Review of the State of Society and Manners of the First Settlers of the West Country*. Clearfield, PA: Clearfield: reprint edition, 2012, pp. 109–110.

4. James Lindgren, "Fall from Grace: *Arming America* and the Bellesiles Scandal," *Yale Law Journal* (June 2002), Vol. 111, p. 2204.

5. Howard Zinn, *A People's History of the United States*. New York: HarperCollins, 1995, p. 23.

6. Robert J. Miller, "The International Law of Colonialism: A Comparative Analysis," in "Symposium of International Law in Indigenous Affairs: The Doctrine of Discovery, the United Nations, and the Organization of Americans States," special issue, *Lewis and Clark Law Review* 15, no. 4 (Winter 2011), 847–922. See also Vine Deloria Jr., *Of Utmost Good Faith*. San Francisco: Straight Arrow Books, 1971, pp. 6–39; Steven T. Newcomb, *Pagans in the Promised Land: Decoding the Doctrine of Christian Discovery*. Golden, CO: Fulcrum, 2008.

7. Domestication of plants took place around the globe in seven locales during approximately the same period, around 8500 BC. Three of the seven were in the Americas, all based on corn: the Valley of Mexico and Central America (Mesoamerica); the South-Central Andes in South America; and eastern North America. The other original agricultural centers were the Tigris-Euphrates and Nile River systems, Sub-Saharan Africa, the Yellow River of northern China, and the Yangtze River of southern China.

8. Hogeland, *Autumn of the Black Snake*, pp. 19–44.

9. Walter Johnson, *River of Dark Dreams: Slavery and Empire in the Cotton Kingdom*. Cambridge, MA: Belknap Press, 2013, p. 32.

CHAPTER TWO

1. Sherman Alexie, *You Don't Have to Say You Love Me*. New York: Little Brown, 2017, p. 297.

2. John Grenier, *The First Way of War, 1607-1814*. New York: Cambridge University Press, 2005, p. 10.

3. Richard Slotkin, *The Fatal Environment: The Myth of the Frontier*

in the Age of Industrialization, 1800–1890. New York: Harper Perennial, 1994, p. 53.

4. Grenier, *First Way of War*, pp. 5, 10.

5. Ibid., p. 1.

6. Bernard Bailyn, *Barbarous Years: The Peopling of British North America: The Conflict of Civilizations, 1600–1675.* New York: Alfred A. Knopf, 2012.

7. Grenier, *First Way of War,* pp. 29–34, 36–37, 39.

8. Ibid., pp. 192–93.

9. Ibid., pp. 40–41, 205.

10. Barbara Cutter, "The Female Indian Killer Memorialized: Hannah Duston and the Nineteenth-Century Feminization of American Violence," *The Journal of Women's History*, 2008, Vol. 20: No. 2.

11. Grenier, *First Way of War,* pp. 221–22.

12. Ibid., pp. 4–5, 7.

13. Ibid., p. 12.

14. Ibid., pp. 223–24.

15. Max Boot, *The Savage Wars of Peace: Small Wars and the Rise of American Power.* New York: Basic Books, 2002.

16. Grenier, *First Way of War*, p. 14.

17. Ronald T. Takaki, *A Different Mirror: A History of Multicultural America.* New York: Little, Brown, 1993, pp. 85–86

18. Richard Slotkin, *Gunfighter Nation: The Myth of the Frontier in Twentieth-Century America.* New York: Atheneum Macmillan, 1992, pp. 455–457.

19. Gary Clayton Anderson, *The Conquest of Texas: Ethnic Cleansing in the Promised Land, 1820–1875.* Norman: University of Oklahoma Press, 2005.

20. Kaplan, Robert D. *Imperial Grunts: The American Military on the Ground.* New York: Random House, 2005, pp. 8–10.

21. Dexter Filkins, "James Mattis, A Warrior in Washington," *The New Yorker*, May 28, 2017.

22. Grenier, *First Way of War*, p. 222.

CHAPTER THREE

1. See: Michelle Alexander, *The New Jim Crow: Mass Incarceration in the Age of Colorblindness.* New York: The New Press, 2011.

2. Mumia Abu-Jamal, *To Protect and Serve Who?* San Francisco: City Lights/Open Media Series, 2015.

3. Sally E. Hadden, *Slave Patrols: Law and Violence in Virginia and the Carolinas.* Cambridge: Harvard University Press, 2001, p. 2.

4. See: Gerald Horne, *The Counter-Revolution of 1776: Slave Resistance and the Origins of the United States of America.* New York: NYU Press, 2014, pp. 23–42.

5. Hadden, *Slave Patrols*, pp. 11–12, 15, 24.

6. Ibid., pp. 25–28.

7. Ibid., pp. 32–35.

8. Ibid., pp. 39–40.

9. From Edward Cantwell's 1860 judicial hornbook *The Practice at Law in North Carolina:* Hadden, *Slave Patrols*, p. 105.

10. The assumption that poor white men dominate gun ownership and violence remains current, when, in fact, those who make less than $25,000 a year are much less likely to own guns. See: Lois Beckett, "Gun Inequality: US study charts rise of hardcore super owners," *The Guardian*, September 19, 2016. Accessed July 29, 2017: www.theguardian.com/us-news/2016/sep/19/us-gun-ownership-survey

11. Hadden, *Slave Patrols*, pp. 71–72, 102–103.

12. Walter Johnson, *River of Dark Dreams: Slavery and Empire in the Cotton Kingdom.* Cambridge: Harvard University Press, 2013, pp. 222–223.

13. Ibid., pp. 234–35

14. Ned Sublette and Constance Sublette, *The American Slave Coast: A History of the Slave-Breeding Industry,* Chicago, IL: Chicago Review Press, 2015, p. 133, quoting Kathleen M. Brown, *Good Wives, Nasty Wenches, and Anxious Patriarchs: Gender, Race, and Power in Colonial Virginia.* Chapel Hill: University of North Carolina Press, 1996, p. 177.

15. See: Pamela D. Bridgewater, "Un/Re/Dis Covering Slave Breeding in the Thirteenth Amendment Jurisprudence," *Washington and Lee Journal of Civil Rights and Social* Justice, Vol. 7, Issue 1, 2001: pp. 12–44. Accessed July 27, 2017: http://scholarlycommons.law.wlu.edu/cgi/viewcontent.cgi?article=1099&context=crsj

16. Sublette and Sublette, *The American Slave Coast*, p. 312.

17. Gary Clayton Anderson, *The Conquest of Texas: Ethnic Cleansing in the Promised Land, 1820–1875.* Norman: University of Oklahoma Press, 2005, pp. 238–39, 151. Also see: Robert M. Utley, *Lone Star Justice: The First Century of the Texas Rangers*, New York: Berkley/Penguin, 2003, and Utley, *Lone Star Lawmen: The Second Century of the Texas Rangers*, New York: Berkley/Penguin, 2008.

18. Anderson, The Conquest of Texas, pp. 198–202, 204–205.

19. Hadden, *Slave Patrols*, p. 205.

20. See: Boyd Cothran, *Remembering the Modoc War: Redemptive Violence and the Making of American Innocence.* Chapel Hill: University of North Carolina Press, 2014. Also see: Benjamin Madley, *An American Genocide: The United States and the California Indian Catastrophe, 1846-1873.* New Haven CT: Yale University Press, 2016.

21. Ibid., p. 206.

22. Ibid., pp. 208–209.

23. Malcolm Harris, "The Future of the United States," a review essay of Sublette and Sublette, *The American Slave Coast*, in *Pacific Standard Magazine*, January 26, 2016. Accessed July 29, 2017: https://psmag. com/a-future-history-of-the-united-states-2965a114f8ee#.6t82shj6j

24. Hadden, p. 216.

25. Hadden, p. 219.

26. Mike Davis, *City of Quartz: Excavating the Future of Los Angeles.* New York: Vintage Books, 1990, Chapter Four.

27. Saul Cornell and Eric M. Ruben, "The Slave-State Origins of Modern Gun Rights," *The Atlantic*, September 30, 2015. Accessed October 16, 2017: https://www.theatlantic.com/politics/archive/2015/09/the-origins-of-public-carry-jurisprudence-in-the-slave-south/407809/

CHAPTER FOUR

1. "Jesse James" or "The Ballad of Jesse James" (traditional, ca. 1882).

2. Written by Robbie Robertson, Copyright © Warner/Chappell Music, Inc.

3. Ralph J. Gleason, *Rolling Stone*, October 1969, quoted in Peter Viney, "The Night They Drove Old Dixie Down," *Jawbone*, Issue 5, Winter 1997, online at: http://theband.hiof.no/articles/dixie_viney_old.html

4. In the 1960s, a distinguished leftist British historian, the late Eric Hobsbawm, famously created the concept of the "social bandit," and included Jesse James as an example of a Robin Hood type. The popularity of his work on the outlaw as a social bandit, given his left politics, may have contributed to the revival in 1960s culture of the mythology of an earlier era. See: Hobsbawm, *Primitive Rebels*, New York: W.W. Norton, 1965; and Hobsbawm, *Bandits* (1969), New York: The New Press; Revised ed., 2000.

5. Forrest Carter, *The Rebel Outlaw: Josey Wales*, 1972; reprinted as *Gone to Texas*, New York: Delacorte, 1975; reprinted New York: Dell, 1980.

6. Forrest Carter, *The Education of Little Tree*, New York: Delacorte Press, 1976; published in a new edition as *The Education of Little Tree: A True Story by Forrest Carter*, Albuquerque: University of New Mexico Press, 1985.

7. "Is Forrest Carter Really Asa Carter? Only Josey Wales May Know for Sure," *New York Times*, August 26, 1976. Accessed September 10, 2017: www.nytimes.com/1976/08/26/archives/is-forrest-carter-really-asa-carter-only-josey-wales-may-know-for.html

8. Matthew Christopher Hulbert, *The Ghosts of Guerrilla Memory: How Civil War Bushwhackers Became Gunslingers in the American West.* Athens: University of Georgia Press, 2016, p. 6. Hulbert argues that the Confederate Missouri guerrillas became a symbolic vanguard of U.S. counterinsurgent wars of conquest in the West following the Civil War. In doing so, he contributes to an understanding of the normalization of guns, the revolver in particular, in U.S. American culture.

9. Ibid., pp. 7–19.

10. Ibid., p. 57. In comparison, the eleven states that made up the Confederacy had a population of 9 million, more than 3 million being enslaved Africans. Seventy-six percent of the settlers owned no slaves, while 24 percent did. Seventeen percent of slavers owned one to nine slaves, and only 6.5 percent owned more than ten. Ten percent of the settlers who owned no slaves were also landless. See: "Selected Statistics on Slavery in the United States," *Causes of the Civil War:* www.civilwar-causes.org/stat.htm. Accessed December 10, 2013.

11. T.J. Stiles, *Jesse James: Last Rebel of the Civil War.* New York: Knopf, 2002, p. 81.

12. Thomas Goodrich, *Bloody Dawn: The Story of the Lawrence Massacre.* Kent, OH: Kent State University Press, 1991, pp. 43–45.

13. Beccy Tanner, "150 years later, Quantrill's raid on Lawrence still stirs deep emotions on both sides," *Wichita Eagle*, August 17, 2013. Accessed July 30, 2017: www.kansas.com/news/local/news-columns-blogs/the-story-of-kansas/article1121021.html

14. Ibid.

15. Ibid.

16. John Newman Edwards, *Noted Guerrillas*, 1877, quoted in Hulbert, *Ghosts of Guerrilla Memory*, p. 53.

17. Hulbert, *Ghosts of Guerrilla Memory*, pp. 50–53.

18. Ibid., p. 64.

19. Ibid., p. 183.

20. Ibid., 183–84. Belle Starr was assassinated in 1889 at age 39, not far from where she lived at "Youngers' Bend" in the Cherokee Nation near the Arkansas border.

21. Ibid., pp. 184–85.

22. Carl Degler, *Out of Our Past.* New York: Harper, 1959, p. 511. Samuel Langhorne Clemens, better know as Mark Twain, was a child of this migration, and his family was quite similar to that of Jesse James, who was twelve years younger. Clemens's mother was from Kentucky, his father from a wealthy slaver family in Virginia, both of Scots-Irish heritage. Clemens was born in 1835 in Florida, Missouri, and when he was five years old the family moved to Hannibal, Missouri, where he grew up. His family always owned or leased enslaved Africans; Clemens had an enslaved woman nanny. He escaped the Missouri-Kansas border war of the 1850s, moved to New York City at age eighteen, and made New York his home most of the rest of his life, except during the Civil War, when he lived in Nevada. In 1869, he married into a family of abolitionists and became friends with many of the illustrious ones, such as Harriet Beecher Stowe. His publishing career and fame followed in the late 1870s and through 1910.

23. Richard Slotkin, *Regeneration Through Violence: The Mythology of the American Frontier, 1600-1860.* Middletown CT: Wesleyan University Press, 1973, p. 42.

24. Stiles, *Jesse James: Last Rebel of the Civil War.*

25. Ibid., p. 393.

26. Richard Maxwell Brown, *No Duty to Retreat: Violence and Values in American Society.* New York: Oxford University Press, 1991, pp. 39–86.

27. Hulbert, *Ghosts of Guerrilla Memory*, p. 82.

CHAPTER FIVE

1. "Gun Ownership Trends and Demographics," U.S. Politics and Policy Section 3, Washington, DC: Pew Research Center, March 12, 2013.

2. Norman Mailer, *The Naked and the Dead: 50th Anniversary Edition Paperback.* New York: Picador, 2000, p. 156.

3. Richard Slotkin, *The Fatal Environment: The Myth of the Frontier in the Age of Industrialization, 1800-1890.* New York: Atheneum, 1985, p. 81.

4. Wallace Stegner, *Where the Bluebird Sings to the Lemonade Springs: Living and Writing in the West.* New York: Random House, 1992, pp. 71–72.

5. Slotkin. *Regeneration through Violence*, pp. 394–95.

6. John Bakeless, *Daniel Boone: Master of the Wilderness*. Originally published 1939, reprinted University of Nebraska Press, 1989: pp. 38–39.

7. Slotkin. *Gunfighter Nation*, pp. 49–51. For Roosevelt's views on eugenics and class, see Nancy Isenberg, *White Trash: The 400-Year Untold History of Class in America.* New York: Viking, 2016, pp. 188–194.

8. Founding Father Alexander Hamilton was married to Elizabeth Schuyler and managed the buying and selling of the family's enslaved Africans.

9. H.W. Brands, *TR: The Last Romantic.* New York: Basic Books, 1997, p. 126.

10. Slotkin, *Gunfighter Nation*, p. 37.

11. Ibid., pp. 41–42.

12. Daniel Hayes, "Donald Trump Takes Aim," *New York Times: Opinion Pages*, August 20, 2016. Accessed July 28, 2017: www.nytimes.com/2016/08/21/opinion/campaign-stops/donald-trump-takes-aim.html?_r=0

13. Ibid.

14. Robert Schenkkan, *The Kentucky Cycle.* New York: Dramatists Play Service Inc., 1994.

15. Ibid., author's note, p. 9.

16. Bobbie Ann Mason, "Recycling Kentucky," *The New Yorker*, November 1, 1993, p. 56.

17. Ibid., pp. 59–62.

18. Ibid.

19. Ibid., p. 62.

20. Daniel Hayes, "Why I Hunt," in Daniel Hayes, ed., *Guns* (Kindle edition), Thought Catalog: Amazon Digital Services LLC, 2016.

21. Ibid.

CHAPTER SIX

1. See: Cecilia Elizabeth O'Leary, *To Die For: The Paradox of American Patriotism.* Princeton, NJ; Princeton University Press, 1999.

2. A fetish is an object believed to embody supernatural or symbolic powers, a man-made object that gives the owner power over others. Sigmund Freud, in his 1927 essay "On Fetishism," retooled the term:

"In all the cases the meaning and purpose of the fetish turned out under analysis to be the same. . . . The fetish is a penis-substitute . . . for a particular quite special penis that had been extremely important in early childhood but was afterwards lost." Accessed July 28, 2017: www.scribd.com/doc/31127300/Freud-Fetishism-1927e#scribd.

3. Fredric Jameson aptly calls the U.S. Constitution a "formational fetish." Fredric Jameson, *An American Utopia: Dual Power and the Universal Army*. London, New York: Verso Books, 2016, p. 67.

4. Garry Wills, "A Nation Captive to the Gun," *Boston Globe*, June 15, 2016. Accessed July 28, 2017: www.bostonglobe.com/opinion/2016/06/14/nation-captive-the-gun/eVN6Kh8hVhodxxMTZnrtBM/story.html

5. "'Full-spectrum dominance' is the key term in 'Joint Vision 2020,' the blueprint DoD will follow in the future." Jim Garamone, American Forces Press Service, "Joint Vision 2020 Emphasizes Full-spectrum Dominance," DoD News, June 2, 2000. Accessed July 22, 2017: http://archive.defense.gov/news/newsarticle.aspx?id=45289

6. Donald Harman Akenson, *God's Peoples: Covenant and Land in South Africa, Israel, and Ulster*. Montreal: McGill-Queen's University Press, 1991, pp. 151–82, 227–62, 311–48.

7. Ibid., pp. 30–31, 73–74.

8. Ibid., p. 112.

9. See: Perry Miller, *Errand in the Wilderness*, Cambridge, MA: Harvard University Press, 1956; and Sarah Vowell, *The Wordy Shipmates*, New York: Riverhead, 2008.

10. Akenson, *God's Peoples*, p. 118.

11. Thomas F. Rzeznik, *Church and Estate: Religion and Wealth in Industrial-Era Philadelphia*. State College, PA: Penn State University, 2013.

12. "Second Amendment," NRA-Institute for Legislative Action. Accessed July 28, 2017: www.nraila.org/second-amendment/

13. *District of Columbia v. Heller*, 554 U.S. 570 (2008). Accessed July 28, 2017: https://supreme.justia.com/cases/federal/us/554/570/

14. Jeffrey M. Jones, "Americans in Agreement With Supreme Court on Gun Rights," Gallup, June 26, 2008. Accessed July 29, 2017: www.gallup.com/poll/108394/americans-agreement-supreme-court-gun-rights.aspx

15. Robert H. Bork, "Neutral Principles and Some First Amendment Problems," *Indiana Law Journal*: 47:1 (Fall 1971). Accessed July 27, 2017: http://digitalcommons.law.yale.edu/cgi/viewcontent.cgi?article=4149&context=fss_papers

16. Claudia Luther, "Bork Says State Gun Laws Constitutional," *Los Angeles Times*, March 15, 1989, p. B5. Accessed October 16, 2017: http://articles.latimes.com/1989-03-15/local/me-587_1_state-gun-laws-constitutional

17. National Archives, "Timeline of Events Leading to the Brown v. Board of Education Decision, 1954." Accessed July 27, 2017: www.archives.gov/education/lessons/brown-v-board/timeline.html

18. See: Rick Perlstein, *Before the Storm: Barry Goldwater and the Unmaking of the American Consensus*. New York: Hill and Wang, 2001.

19. Joel Achenbach, Scott Higham, and Sari Horwitz, "How NRA's True Believers Converted a Marksmanship Group into a Mighty Gun Lobby," *Washington Post*, January 12, 2013. Accessed July 27, 2017: www.washingtonpost.com/politics/how-nras-true-believers-converted-a-marksmanship-group-into-a-mighty-gun-lobby/2013/01/12/51c62288-59b9-11e2-88d0-c4cf65c3ad15_story.html

20. Mark Ames, "From 'Operation Wetback' to Newtown: Tracing the Hick Fascism of The NRA," *Pando*, December 17, 2012. Accessed July 27, 2017: www.nsfwcorp.com/dispatch/newtown/

21. Mark Ames, "A Brief History of American Gun Nuts," *Pando*, June 26, 2015. Accessed July 27, 2017: https://pando.com/2015/06/26/brief-history-american-gun-nuts/.

22. "Trump Tells N.R.A. Convention, 'I Am Going to Come Through for You.'" *New York Times*, April 28, 2107. Accessed July 27, 2017: www.nytimes.com/2017/04/28/us/politics/donald-trump-nra.html?_r=0

23. George Zornick, "Trump and the NRA," *The Nation*, July 17, 2017, Vol. 305, Issue 2.

CHAPTER SEVEN

1. Hulbert, *Ghosts of Guerrilla Memory*, p. 5.

2. See: Bonnie Berkowitz, Lazaro Gamio, Denise Lu, Kevin Uhrmacher and Todd Lindeman, "The Math of Mass Shootings," *Washington Post*, July 27, 2016. These 128 events do not include gun shootings during a robbery, spree shootings (shooting two or more victims in a short time in multiple locations), or gang deaths, nor domestic homicide or suicide. Accessed July 28, 2017: www.washingtonpost.com/graphics/national/mass-shootings-in-america/. See also the database of mass shootings compiled by *Mother Jones* magazine, which is frequently updated. Accessed July 27, 2017: www.motherjones.com/politics/2012/12/mass-shootings-mother-jones-full-data/

3. Sharon LaFraniere, Sarah Cohen and Richard A. Oppel Jr., "How Often Do Mass Shoootings Occur? On the Average, Every Day, Records Show," *New York Times*, December 2, 2015. Accessed July 28, 2017: www.nytimes.com/2015/12/03/us/how-often-do-mass-shootings-occur-on-average-every-day-records-show.html?_r=0

4. Jane Mayer, "The Link Between Domestic Violence and Mass Shootings," *The New Yorker*, June 16, 2017. Accessed September 10, 2017: www.newyorker.com/news/news-desk/the-link-between-domestic-violence-and-mass-shootings-james-hodgkinson-steve-scalise

5. Monte Akers, Nathan Akers, and Dr. Roger Friedman, *Tower Sniper: The Terror of America's First Campus Active Shooter*. Houston: John M. Hardy Publishing, 2016. See also: Gary M. Lavergne, *A Sniper in the Tower: The Charles Whitman Murders*. Denton, Texas: University of North Texas Press, 1997.

6. Lawrence Wright, "America's Future Is Texas," *The New Yorker*, July 10 & 17, 2017. Accessed July 28, 2017: www.newyorker.com/magazine/2017/07/10/americas-future-is-texas

7. Ibid.

8. "San Ysidro Massacre," *San Diego Union-Tribune*, July 19, 1984. Accessed July 29, 2017: www.sandiegouniontribune.com/sdut-san-ysidro-massacre-1984jul19-story.html. For a biography of the shooter, James Huberty, see: http://murderpedia.org/male.H/h/huberty-james.htm

9. Richard Woodbury, "Ten Minutes in Hell," *Time*, October 28, 1991.

10. Paula Chin, "A Texas Massacre," *People*, November 4, 1991. Accessed October 16, 2017: http://people.com/archive/a-texas-massacre-vol-36-no-17/. A similar incident of a gunman targeting women took place two years earlier in Montreal, Quebec, at a technical school engineering class, killing twenty-eight people, half of them women. Before he began shooting, the gunman announced that he was fighting feminism and called the women "a bunch of feminists." He left a suicide note blaming women for ruining his life, including a list of nineteen women he wanted to kill. Barry Came, D. Burke, G. Ferzoco, B. O'Farreli, B. Wallace, "Montreal Massacre: Railing Against Feminists," *Maclean's Magazine*, December 18, 1989.

11. Mark Follman, Gavin Aronsen, and Deanna Pan, "US Mass Shootings, 1982–2016: Data From Mother Jones' Investigation," *Mother Jones*, June 12, 2016. Accessed July 28, 2017: www.motherjones.com/politics/2012/12/mass-shootings-mother-jones-full-data/

12. A year and a half before the Newtown massacre, a right-wing Norwegian, Anders Behring Breivik, heavily armed and disguised as a policeman, took a ferry to a small island near Oslo where a summer camp for some six hundred teenagers from the youth wing of a left political organization was in session, killing 69 and wounding 110, the youngest fatality being fourteen years old.

13. Chuck Haga, "Family: Teen had 'good relationship' with grandfather he killed," *Minneapolis-St. Paul Star Tribune*, March 25, 2005; Jeremy Lennard, "Ten Dead in US School Shooting," *The Guardian*, March 22, 2005. See also: Jodi A. Byrd, "'Living My Native Life Deadly': Red Lake, Ward Churchill, and the Discourses of Competing Genocides," *American Indian Quarterly* 31 (Spring 2007): pp. 310–332.

14. Daniel N. Paul, "We Were Not the Savages," August 31, 2008. Accessed July 22, 2017: www.danielnpaul.com/NativeAmericansDemonized.html

15. Before going on the killing rampage, Cho mailed a video of his manifesto to NBC News headquarters in New York: www.nbcnews.com/id/18187368/ns/us_news-crime_and_courts/t/va-tech-killers-strange-manifesto. The video can be seen here: www.youtube.com/watch?v=JmE4t6BnEhQ

16. Washington Post Staff, "How the Las Vegas Strip Shooting Unfolded," , October 3, 2017. Accessed October 9, 2017: www.washingtonpost.com/graphics/2017/national/las-vegas-shooting/?utm_term=.2575b4799866

17. "Las Vegas Shooting: N.R.A. Supports New Rules on 'Bump Stock' Devices, *New York Times*, October 5, 2017. Accessed October 9, 2017: www.nytimes.com/2017/10/05/us/las-vegas-shooting.html?hp&action=click&pgtype=Homepage&clickSource=story-heading&module=a-lede-package-region&region=top-news&WT.nav=top-news

18. Grenier, *First Way of War*, pp. 5, 10.

19. Andrew J. Bacevich, *The New American Militarism: How Americans Are Seduced by War*. New York: Oxford University Press, 2005.

20. Jeremy Herb, "Congress proposes defense budget $37 billion higher than Trump's," *CNN.com*, June 22, 2017. Accessed July 28, 2017: www.cnn.com/2017/06/22/politics/congress-trump-defense-budget/index.html

21. See: Iain Overton, *The Way of the Gun: A Bloody Journey into the World of Firearms*. New York: Harper, 2016. For a review of Overton's findings, see: C.J. Chivers, "How Many Guns Did the U.S. Lose

Track of in Iraq and Afghanistan? Hundreds of Thousands," *New York Times Magazine*, August 24, 2016. Accessed July 28, 2017: www.nytimes.com/2016/08/23/magazine/how-many-guns-did-the-us-lose-track-of-in-iraq-and-afghanistan-hundreds-of-thousands.html

22. Overton, *Way of the Gun*, p. ix.

23. Thom Shanker, "U.S. Sold $40 Billion in Weapons in 2015, Topping Global Market," *New York Times*, December 26, 2016. Accessed July 27, 2017: www.nytimes.com/2016/12/26/us/politics/united-states-global-weapons-sales.html?_r=0

24. SIRPI, "Increase in arms transfers driven by demand in the Middle East and Asia, says SIRPI," February 20, 2017. Accessed July 27, 2017: www.sipri.org/media/press-release/2017/increase-arms-transfers-driven-demand-middle-east-and-asia-says-sipri

25. United Nations Office for Disarmament Affairs, The Arms Trade Treaty (ATT). Accessed July 27, 2017: www.un.org/disarmament/convarms/att/

CHAPTER EIGHT

1. When a hollow-point bullet strikes a person, the bullet expands on penetration, opening up like a parachute, causing far more damage to tissue, organs, and arteries. Michael S. Schmidt, "Background Check Flaw Let Dylann Roof Buy Gun, FBI Says," *New York Times*, July 10, 2015. Accessed July 27, 2017: www.nytimes.com/2015/07/11/us/background-check-flaw-let-dylann-roof-buy-gun-fbi-says.html?_r=0

2. "Donald Trump, Jr. Speaks at Neshoba Fair," *The Clarion-Ledger*, July 27, 2016.

3. Ibid.

4. From the *Christian Posse Comitatus Newsletter,* quoted in Kenneth S. Stern, *A Force upon the Plain: The American Militia Movement and the Politics of Hate*. New York: Simon and Schuster, 1996, p. 50.

5. Alexander Reid Ross, *Against the Fascist Creep*. Oakland CA: AK Press, 2017.

6. Ibid., p. 2.

7. Ibid., p. 94.

8. Ibid., pp. 95–96.

9. Ibid., pp. 97–98.

10. Ibid., pp. 206, 254.

11. Ibid., pp. 96–101.

12. Federal Bureau of Investigation (FBI), *White Supremacist*

Infiltration of Law Enforcement. Washington DC: FBI Counterterrorism Division, October 17, 2006. http://s3.documentcloud.org/documents/402521/doc-26-white-supremacist-infiltration.pdf

13. Samuel V. Jones, "FBI's Warning of White Supremacists Infiltrating Law Enforcement Nearly Forgotten," *The Grio*, May 12, 2015. Accessed July 28, 2017: http://thegrio.com/2015/05/12/fbi-white-supremacists-law-enforcement/

14. Lois Beckett, "Gun Inequality: US study charts rise of hardcore super owners," *The Guardian*, September 19, 2016. Accessed July 29, 2017: www.theguardian.com/us-news/2016/sep/19/us-gun-ownership-survey

15. Daniel Trotta, "U.S. Military Battling White Supremacists, Neo-Nazis In Its Own Ranks," *Huffington Post*, October 21, 2012. Accessed July 28, 2017: www.huffingtonpost.com/2012/08/21/us-army-white-supremacists_n_1815137.html

16. Ibid.

17. Matt Kennard, *Irregular Army: How the US Military Recruited Neo-Nazis, Gang Members, and Criminals to Fight the War on Terror.* New York: Verso Books, 2012, p. 13.

18. Robert F. Williams, *Negroes with Guns.* Eastford, CT: Martino Fine Books, 2013; reprint of the original 1962 book. Text accessible at: https://libcom.org/files/Robert%20Franklin%20Williams%20-%20Negroes%20with%20guns.pdf

19. Charles E. Cobb Jr., *This Nonviolent Stuff'll Get You Killed: How Guns Made the Civil Rights Movement Possible.* Durham, NC: Duke University Press, 2015.

20. "Armed Black Panthers Invade Capitol," *Sacramento Bee*, May 4, 1967. Accessed October 16, 2017: http://www.sacbee.com/news/local/history/article148667224.html

21. Caroline E. Light, *Stand Your Ground: A History of America's Love Affair with Lethal Self-Defense.* Boston: Beacon Press, 2017, p. 128.

22. Ibid., p. 165.

23. David Cay Johnston, "William Pierce, 69, Neo-Nazi Leader, Dies," *New York Times*, July 24, 2002. Accessed July 29, 2017: www.nytimes.com/2002/07/24/us/william-pierce-69-neo-nazi-leader-dies.html?_r=0

24. The full text of *The Turner Diaries* can be read free online. Accessed July 29, 2017: https://docs.google.com/file/d/0B0xb4crOvCgTSk9CcXRLYkN4TUU/view

CHAPTER NINE

1. Emma Pettit, "The New Gun-Violence Scholars," *Chronicle of Higher Education*, August 22, 2016.

2. Joe Helm, "Recounting a day of rage, hate, violence, and death," *Washington Post*, August 14, 2017. Accessed October 9, 2017: www.washingtonpost.com/graphics/2017/local/charlottesville-timeline/ ; "Unrest in Virginia: Clashes over a Show of White Nationalism in Charlottesville Turn Deadly," *Time Magazine*, August 14, 2017. Accessed October 9, 2017: time.com/charlottesville-white-nationalist-rally-clashes/; Christina Caron, "Heather Heyer, Charlottesville Victim, Is Recalled as 'a Strong Woman," *New York Times*, August 13, 2017: www.nytimes.com/2017/08/13/us/heather-heyer-charlottesville-victim. html; "Trump says both sides to blame for Charlottesville violence," YouTube, August 15, 2017. Accessed October 9, 2017: www.youtube. com/watch?v=Jlh-n8EKvoZU.

3. See: Mark Bray, *Antifa: The Anti-Fascist Handbook*, New York: Melville House, 2017; Alexander Reid-Ross, *Against the Fascist Creep*.

4. Colleen Flaherty, "Don't 'Go There,'" *Inside Higher Ed*, February 24, 2016. Accessed July 27, 2017: www.insidehighered.com/news/2016/02/24/u-houston-faculty-senate-suggests-changes-teaching-under-campus-carry?utm_source=Inside+Higher+Ed&utm_campaign=183bc9e3a3-DNU20160224&utm_medium=email&utm_term=0_1fcbc04421-183bc9e3a3-197425449#.Vs8zo9rq4zM.mailto

5. Pamela Haag, *The Gunning of America: Business and the Making of American Gun Culture*. New York: Basic Books, 2016.

6. Ibid., p. x

7. Ibid., p. xi.

8. Ibid., pp. xi, xii.

9. Ibid., p. xii.

10. It is indeed the case that Walmart is a major driver of gun sales in the United States. See: George Zornick, "How Walmart Helped Make the Newtown Shooter's AR-15 the Most Popular Assault Weapon in America," *The Nation*, December 9, 2012. Zornick writes, "A massive recent spike in gun sales has boosted Walmart's flagging profits, making it the top seller of firearms and ammunition nationwide." Accessed July 21, 2017: www.thenation.com/article/how-walmart-helped-make-newtown-shooters-ar-15-most-popular-assault-weapon-america/. Also see: MJ Lee, "Why Walmart will keep selling guns," *CNN*, June 25, 2015. Accessed July 24, 2017: www.cnn.com/2015/06/25/politics/walmart-guns-confederate-flag/index.html

11. Haag, *Gunning of America*, pp. 179, 183.

12. Michael A. Bellesiles, *Arming America: The Origins of a National Gun Culture*. New York: Alfred A. Knopf, 2000, p. 110. After Knopf halted publication of the book, it was picked up by Soft Skull Press, Berkeley, CA, in 2003 and remains available.

13. Garry Wills, "Spiking the Gun Myth," *New York Times Book Review*, September 10, 2000; Edmund S. Morgan, "In Love with Guns," *New York Review of Books*, October 19, 2000.

14. Nick Sanchez, "25 Best Charlton Heston 'Gun Freedom' Quotes," *Newsmax*, July 22, 2017. Accessed July 24, 2017: www.newsmax.com/TheWire/charlton-heston-gun-quotes-top/2015/10/23/id/697700/

15. James Lindgren, "Fall from Grace: *Arming America* and the Bellesiles Scandal," *Yale Law Journal* (June 2002), Vol. 111, pp. 2234–2249.

16. Ibid., p. 2197.

17. Ibid., pp. 2208–2210.

18. Ibid., pp. 2205–06. Also see: Robert H. Churchill, "Guns and the Politics of History," *Reviews in American History*, 2001, 29: p. 329.

19. Lindgren, "Fall from Grace," p. 2232.

20. Ibid., p. 2197.

21. Jon Wiener, "Fire at Will," *The Nation*, October 17, 2002. Accessed October 16, 2017: https://www.thenation.com/article/fire-will/

22. Ibid.

23. Official announcement by the Columbia University Board of Trustees, December 13, 2002. See full text at: http://historynewsnetwork.org/article/1157. Accessed July 21, 2017.

24. Jon Wiener, *Historians in Trouble: Plagiarism, Fraud, and Politics in the Ivory Tower*. New York: New Press, 2005.

25. Ibid.

26. "Swiftboating" refers to the right-wing attack on Senator John Kerry when he was the Democratic candidate for president in 2004. Kerry had served as a Swift Boat captain in the Vietnam War, and his campaign was presenting him as a war hero who could better handle the ongoing wars in Afghanistan and Iraq than President George W. Bush, his opponent. However, Kerry, who had received the Congressional Medal of Honor for his combat service, returned from Vietnam strongly against the war and joined with other Vietnam veterans in protests, including tossing their medals over the White House fence. Vietnam War veteran diehards and the right-wing militarists in general hated Kerry nearly as much as they hated Jane Fonda, and their vicious and perva-

sive attacks and lies about Kerry during the campaign came to be called "swiftboating."

27. Scott McLemee, "Amazing Disgrace," *Inside Higher Ed*, May 19, 2010. Accessed July 21, 2017: www.insidehighered.com/views/2010/05/19/amazing-disgrace

28. Library of Congress. Accessed July 24, 2017: www.loc.gov/item/ca0959/

29. CBS Films, *Winchester*, starring Helen Mirren, scheduled release date: February 23, 2018. Accessed July 24, 2017: www.imdb.com/title/tt1072748/

30. Haag, *Gunning of America*, pp. 285–289.

CONCLUSION

1. Clare Foran, "The House Democrats' Sit-In Comes to an End," *The Atlantic*, June 23, 2016. Accessed July 21, 2017: www.theatlantic.com/politics/archive/2016/06/house-democrats-sit-in-guns/488444/

2. "The Terrorist Screening Center, a multi-agency center administered by the FBI, is the U.S. Government's consolidated counterterrorism watchlisting component and is responsible for the management and operation of the Terrorist Screening Database, commonly known as 'the watchlist.'" Accessed July 24, 2017: www.fbi.gov/about/leadership-and-structure/national-security-branch/tsc

3. Phillip Bump, "The Problem with Banning Guns for People on the No-Fly List," *Washington Post*, June 13, 2016. Accessed July 21, 2017: www.washingtonpost.com/news/the-fix/wp/2015/12/07/the-no-fly-list-is-a-terrible-tool-for-gun-control-in-part-because-it-is-a-terrible-tool/

4. Emily Richmond, "Civic Lessons From the House Democrats' Sit-In," *The Atlantic*, June 28, 2016. Accessed July 21, 2017: www.theatlantic.com/education/archive/2016/06/civics-lessons-from-the-house-democrats-sit-in/489167/. Also see: Phyllis Bennis, "The House Sit-In Would've Been More Powerful If It Rejected 'No Fly, No Buy,'" *Foreign Policy in Focus*, June 23, 2016. Accessed July 21, 2017: http://fpif.org/house-sit-wouldve-powerful-rejected-no-fly-no-buy/

5. Melissa Davey, "Australia's gun laws stopped mass shootings and reduced homicides, study finds," *The Guardian*, June 22, 2016. Accessed July 21, 2017: www.theguardian.com/world/2016/jun/23/australias-gun-laws-stopped-mass-shootings-and-reduced-homicides-study-finds. See also: Simon Chapman, Philip Alpers, and Michael Jones, "Association Between Gun Law Reforms and Intentional Firearm Deaths in Australia,

1979–2013," *JAMA: The Journal of the American Medical Association*, Vol. 316, No. 3, July 19, 2016. Accessed July 24, 2017: http://jama.jamanetwork.com/article.aspx?articleid=2530362

6. Hahrie Han, "Want Gun Control? Learn from the N.R.A.," Opinion section, *New York Times*, October 4, 2017. Accessed October 9, 2017: www.nytimes.com/2017/10/04/opinion/gun-control-nra-vegas.html

7. Jeffrey M. Jones, "Americans in Agreement With Supreme Court on Gun Rights," Gallup, June 16, 2008. Accessed July 21, 2017: www.gallup.com/poll/108394/americans-agreement-supreme-court-gun-rights.aspx

8. Sarah Ellison, "The Civil War that Could Doom the N.R.A.," *Vanity Fair*, June 27, 2016. Accessed October 16, 2017: https://www.vanityfair.com/news/2016/06/the-civil-war-that-could-doom-the-nra. See also: Adam Winkler, *Gunfight: The Battle over the Right to Bear Arms in America*. New York: W.W. Norton, 2013. At its 2016 convention in Louisville, Kentucky, the N.R.A. endorsed Donald Trump, the Republican nominee for president, and Trump addressed the thousands of enthusiastic attendees: Michele Gorman, "Donald Trump and NRA Endorse Each Other," *Newsweek*, May 20, 2016. Accessed July 21, 2017: www.newsweek.com/donald-trump-and-nra-endorse-each-other-462187

9. Mark Ames, *Going Postal: Rage, Murder, and Rebellion: From Reagan's Workplaces to Clinton's Columbine and Beyond*. San Francisco: Soft Skull Press, 2005.

10. Mark Ames, "From 'Operation Wetback' to Newtown: Tracing the Hick Fascism of the NRA," *Pando*, December 17, 2012. Accessed July 21, 2017: www.nsfwcorp.com/dispatch/newtown/

11. Mark Ames, "A Brief History of American Gun Nuts," *Pando.com*, June 26, 2015. Accessed July 28, 2017: https://pando.com/2015/06/26/brief-history-american-gun-nuts/

12. Ibid.

13. Ted Koppel, "Guns, A Family Affair," *CBS Sunday Morning*, March 13, 2016. Accessed July 21, 2017: www.cbsnews.com/news/guns-a-family-affair/. Wyoming is the state with the most firearms per capita (196 per 1,000), three times as many as the next highest (District of Columbia), with more than half the population owning firearms and with one of the highest gun death rates. Accessed July 24, 2017: http://reverbpress.com/politics/firearms-per-capita-by-state/

14. Transcript: Face to Face with Alan Simpson, CBS News, Febru-

ary 23, 2012. Accessed July 21, 2017: www.cbsnews.com/news/transcript-face-to-face-with-alan-simpson/

15. Jessica Chia, "George Zimmerman 'sells Trayvon Martin gun for $250,000 to a mother planning to give it to her son for his birthday' and claims he auctioned it off because he's sick of Hillary Clinton's anti-gun rhetoric," *DailyMail.com*, May 24, 2016. Accessed July 21, 2017: www.dailymail.co.uk/news/article-3607507/George-Zimmerman-sells-gun-250-0000-mother-planning-pistol-son-birthday-claims-launched-auction-s-sick-Hillary-Clinton-s-anti-gun-rhetoric.html

16. Mike McPhate, "George Zimmerman's 3rd Auction for Gun Brings $138,900 High Bid," *New York Times*, May 18, 2016. Accessed July 21, 2017: www.nytimes.com/2016/05/19/us/george-zimmermans-3rd-auction-for-gun-brings-138900-high-bid.html

17. See: Richard Slotkin, *Regeneration Through Violence: The Mythology of the American Frontier, 1600-1860.* Middletown CT: Wesleyan University Press, 1973.

18. See: Nick Turse, *Kill Anything that Moves: The Real American War in Vietnam.* New York: Metropolitan Books, 2013.

19. For photographs and documents, see Arnaldo Dumindin, *Philippine-American War, 1899–1902.* Accessed July 21, 2017: http://philippineamericanwar.webs.com

20. Walter L. Williams, "United States Indian Policy and the Debate over Philippine Annexation: Implications for the Origins of American Imperialism," *Journal of American History* Vol. 66, no. 4 (March 1980): pp. 810–31.

21. Robert Kaplan, *Imperial Grunts: The American Military on the Ground.* New York: Random House, 2005, p. 138.

22. See: Jeremy Kuzmarov, *Modernizing Repression: Police Training and Nation-Building in the American Century.* Amherst: University of Massachusetts Press, 2012.

23. See: Gregorio Selser (Cedric Belfrage, translator), *Sandino.* New York: Monthly Review Books, 1982. Nicaraguans lived under the Somoza family dictatorship for half a century until a new generation, heirs of Sandino's anti-imperialist struggle, overthrew the Somoza dictatorship in 1979. Again, the United States created a counterinsurgency that devastated Nicaragua in the 1980s, forcing the Sandinistas out of power electorally in 1989.

24. See: John Marciano, *The American War in Vietnam, Crime or Commemoration?* New York: Monthly Review Press, 2016. The Pentagon,

under the Obama administration, organized commemorative activities to take place from 2016 to 2025, covering the 50th anniversary of the decade of the war, 1966–1975.

25. Theresa Tuohy, "The U.S. is celebrating the wrong anniversary for the Vietnam War," *Washington Post*, April 27, 2015. Accessed July 24, 2017: www.washingtonpost.com/posteverything/wp/2015/04/27/we-were-already-in-vietnam-before-65-nows-the-wrong-year-to-mark-the-wars-50th-anniversary/?utm_term=.07652a1a7e72

26. Ken Burns and Lynn Novick, *The Vietnam War*, Public Broadcasting System, September 2017. Accessed September 21, 2017: www.pbs.org/kenburns/the-vietnam-war/home/

27. Slotkin, *Gunfighter Nation*, pp. 1–3.

28. Liam Stack, "What We Know About the Standoff in Oregon," *New York Times*, January 3, 2016. Accessed July 21, 2017: www.nytimes.com/interactive/2016/01/04/us/04oregon-listy.html?action=click&contentCollection=US&module=RelatedCoverage&region=EndOfArticle&pgtype=article

29. Jacqueline Keeler, "'It's So Disgusting' Malheur Militia Dug Latrine Trenches Among Sacred Artifacts," *Indian Country Today*, February 17, 2016. Accessed July 21, 2017: indiancountrytodaymedianetwork.com/2016/02/17/its-so-disgusting-malheur-militia-dug-latrine-trenches-among-sacred-artifacts-163454

30. See: Kollibri Terre Sonnenblum, "The Malheur Wildlife Refuge Occupation: A Skirmish Among Colonizers, *CounterPunch*, January 6, 2016. Accessed July 21, 2017: www.counterpunch.org/2016/01/06/the-malheur-wildlife-refuge-occupation-a-skirmish-among-colonizers/

31. Quoted in Daniel Hayes, "Why I Hunt," in Daniel Hayes, ed., *Guns* (Kindle edition), Thought Catalog: Amazon Digital Services LLC, 2016.

INDEX

© Barrie Karp

ABOUT THE AUTHOR

Roxanne Dunbar-Ortiz grew up in rural Oklahoma, the daughter of a tenant farming family. She is the author of many books, including the acclaimed *An Indigenous Peoples' History of the United States*, *Red Dirt: Growing Up Okie*, *Roots of Resistance: A History of Land Tenure in New Mexico*, and *Blood on the Border: A Memoir of the Contra War*. She lives in San Francisco.